The Lucent Library of Historical Eras

Elizabethan England
Primary Sources

Other titles in the Lucent Library of Historical Eras, Elizabethan England, include:

Elizabeth I and Her Court
Great Elizabethan Playwrights
A History of the Elizabethan Theater
Life in Elizabethan London

The Lucent Library of Historical Eras

Elizabethan England
Primary Sources

Clarice Swisher, Editor

LUCENT BOOKS

THOMSON

GALE

San Diego • Detroit • New York • San Francisco • Cleveland • New Haven, Conn. • Waterville, Maine • London • Munich

THOMSON

GALE

© 2003 by Lucent Books. Lucent Books is an imprint of The Gale Group, Inc., a division of Thomson Learning, Inc.

Lucent Books® and Thomson Learning™ are trademarks used herein under license.

For more information, contact
Lucent Books
27500 Drake Rd.
Farmington Hills, MI 48331-3535
Or you can visit our Internet site at http://www.gale.com

LIBRARY OF CONGRESS CATALOGING-IN-PUBLICATION DATA

Primary sources / [compiled] by Clarice Swisher.
     v. cm. — (The Lucent library of historical eras. Elizabethan England)
    Includes bibliographical references and index.
Contents: Elizabeth's court: her persona and her personality—Political and social issues—Entertainment, theaters, and playwrights—Elizabethan language and literature—English life.
    ISBN 1-59018-097-6 (hardback: alk. paper)
    1. Great Britain—History—Elizabeth, 1558–1603—Sources—Juvenile literature. 2. England—Social life and customs—16th century—Sources—Juvenile literature. [1. Great Britain—History—Elizabeth, 1558–1603—Sources. 2. England—Social life and customs—16th century—Sources.] I. Swisher, Clarice, 1933– II. Series.
    DA350 .P76 2003
    942.05'5—dc21
                                     2002013080

Printed in the United States of America

Contents

Foreword

Looking back from the vantage point of the present, history can be viewed as a myriad of intertwining roads paved by human events. Some paths stand out—broad highways whose mileposts, even from a distance of centuries, are clear. The events that propelled the rise to power of Germany's Third Reich, its role in World War II, and its eventual demise, for example, are well defined and documented.

Other roads are less distinct, their route sometimes hidden from view. Modern legislatures may have developed from old tribal councils, for example, but the links between them are indistinct in places, open to discussion and interpretation.

The architecture of civilization—law, religion, art, science, and government—as well as the more everyday aspects of our culture—what we eat, what we wear—all developed along the historical roads and byways. In that progression can be traced every facet of modern life.

A broad look back along these roads reveals that many paths—though of vastly different character—seem to converge at a few critical junctions. These intersections are those great historical eras that echo over the long, steady course of human history, extending beyond the past and into the present.

These epic periods of time are the focus of Lucent's Library of Historical Eras. They shine through the mists of history like beacons, illuminated by a burst of creativity that propels events forward—so bright that we, from thousands of years away, can clearly see the chain of events leading to the present.

Each Lucent Library of Historical Eras consists of a set of books that highlight various aspects of these major eras. For example, the Elizabethan England library features volumes on Queen Elizabeth I and her court, Elizabethan theater, the great playwrights, and everyday life in Elizabethan London.

The mini-library approach allows for the division of each era into its most significant and most interesting parts and the exploration of those parts in depth. Also, social and cultural trends as well as illustrative documents and eyewitness accounts can be prominently featured in individual volumes.

Lucent's Library of Historical Eras presents a wealth of information to young readers. The lively narrative, fully documented primary and secondary source quotations, maps, photographs, sidebars, and annotated bibliographies serve as launching points for class discussion and further research.

In studying the great historical eras, students also develop a better understanding of our own times. What we learn from the past and how we apply it in the present may shape the future and may determine whether our era will be a guiding light to those traveling future roads.

The Reign of Elizabeth I

The Elizabethan era in England lasted for forty-five years. It began on November 17, 1558, with the crowning of Elizabeth Tudor. Elizabeth was only twenty-five years old when she became Queen Elizabeth I, and she remained queen until she died on March 24, 1603.

Although she was the queen, Elizabeth did not rule the country alone. She had the help of her courtiers. These were her personal servants, her advisers, and her state ministers. The courtiers were integral to Elizabeth's rule. They helped her entertain foreign ambassadors and formulate policy concerning matters at home and abroad. The courtiers encouraged Elizabeth to marry, for example, in an effort to form an alliance with another European power.

Although Elizabeth ultimately chose to remain unmarried, her courtiers' advice on this and other issues was always welcomed.

Elizabeth managed her courtiers and ruled her kingdom with grace, style, and manipulation. She dressed in fine clothes and jewels so that she always stood out among the English population. She minimized her personal thoughts and feelings, putting the best interests of England ahead of her own preferences. She manipulated and controlled her servants by keeping them off guard. She demoted and insulted courtiers when she was displeased with them and advanced them to favored positions in her court seemingly on a whim.

The courtiers and public responded to their queen by trying very hard to win her approval. Courtiers lavished praise and affection on her, always trying to please her. English citizens spent money they did not have to prepare their homes for a visit from their queen; Elizabeth made frequent trips, called progresses, to visit her subjects in London and the surrounding countryside.

Elizabeth managed the English court and the English people with success. Documents in this chapter illustrate her interaction with her courtiers, reveal her popularity with the English people, and show the admiration of Elizabethan writers for her.

Editor's Note: These primary source documents reflect the actual spellings and language used during the Elizabethan era. In some cases, authors use the letter "u" for "v" and vice versa. In others, the notations are incomplete or include archaic symbols. We have left the articles in their original form to preserve the authenticity of the documents.

The Coronation of Queen Elizabeth I

Kings and queens of England are crowned in Westminster Abbey, a cathedral built during the tenth century in the heart of London. On November 17, 1558, Elizabeth was crowned there. The coronation chair on which Elizabeth sat during the ceremony has been used in coronations since 1301, when it was made. An anonymous writer describes the crowning ceremony and the religious ceremony that accompanied it.

First her Grace [Elizabeth] sat in a chair of Estate [the coronation chair] in the middle of the Church before the high altar and immediately her Grace was conducted from the said chair and led between two Lords [members of the House of Lords] to be proclaimed by a Bishop, Queen of England, at four places and the trumpets blowing at every proclamation. And imme-diately the Queen's Majesty was brought to the Chair of Estate.

And immediately her Grace was led before the high altar and there sitting a Bishop, the Queen's Majesty kneeling before

The presence of courtiers in the background of this portrait of Queen Elizabeth I reveals their degree of importance to the monarch's rule.

the Bishop kissed the paten [a plate or shallow dish]. Her Grace offered money and the Bishop laid it in the basin and immediately offered a pall of red silk wherein the paten was covered.

And immediately her Highness sat in a chair before the altar there being a Bishop in the pulpit preaching a sermon before the Queen's Majesty and all the Lords spiritual and temporal. And after the sermon done the Bishop bade the beads. Her Grace void out of the chair kneeling and said the Lord's Prayer.

And the Queen's Majesty being newly apparelled came before the altar and leaned upon the cushions, and over her was spread a red silken cloth. And then and there the Bishop annointed her Grace. And that done changing apparel her Grace returned and sat in her chair.

And there was a sword with a girdle put over her and upon one of her shoulders and under the other and so the sword hanging by her side. And after that two garters [bands] upon her hands, and then one crown put the Bishop upon her head, and then trumpets sounding and the Bishop put a ring upon her finger and delivered the scepter in her hand and then after, the Bishop sat a crown upon her head and the trumpets sounding. And after that her Grace offered the sword, and laid it upon the altar and returned, kneeling. And the Bishop reading upon a Book, and she having a scepter and a cross in her hand. And after that her Grace returned to the Chair of Estate.

And then the Bishop put his hand to the Queen's hand and read certain words to her Grace. And then the Lords went up to her Grace kneeling upon their knees and kissed her Grace. And after the Lords had done, the Bishops came one after another kneeling and kissing her Grace.

And after that the Bishop began the Mass, the Queen's Majesty having the scepter in the right hand and the world in the left hand, the epistle read first in Latin, and after that in English. And after that, the Bishop brought her Grace the Gospel, which also was read first in Latin and after in English, and she kissed the words of the gospel. And immediately after her Majesty went to the offering. And before her Grace was borne three naked swords, and a sword in the scabbard. And her Grace kneeling before the altar and kissed the paten, and offered certain money into the basin. And then and there was read to her Grace certain words. And then her Grace returned into her closet [Private Chamber] hearing the consecration of the Mass and her Grace kissed the pax [a tablet decorated with a sacred figure].

And when Mass was done her Grace removed behind the high altar.

C.G. Bayne, ed., "The Coronation of Queen Elizabeth," *English Historical Review,* XXII (1907), 666–71.

The Pressure on Elizabeth to Marry

Throughout Elizabeth's reign, the church, Parliament, and the English people urged her to marry in order to produce an heir. This would ensure succession and advance her for-

eign policy. She had suitors from Spain, Austria, France, Sweden, and Scotland. All hoped to marry Elizabeth and form a powerful alliance with England. Elizabeth used all of her suitors for the advantages they could offer to enhance England's power, sometimes keeping prospects waiting for many years. In the end, she refused them all. In the following message to the queen, Archbishop of Canterbury Matthew Parker expresses a view held by many people: that Elizabeth should be married.

Most sovereign Lady, as in most loyal obedience and duty of allegiance to your Highness, we [the clergy] thought it part of our pastoral office, to be solicitous in that cause which all your loving subjects so daily sigh for and morningly in their prayers desire to appear to their eyes. Marriage we all wish to see your godly affection inclined to, whereby your noble blood might be continued to reign over us to our great joy and comfort, whereby the great fears of ruin of this your ancient empire might be prevented, the destruction of your natural-born subjects avoided. We cannot but fear this continued sterility [her not being married] in your Highness' person to be a great token of God's displeasure toward us. The greatest part of your most assured faithful subjects secretly rejoiceth with thanks to God, to see your reign hitherto so prosperous, the rather for the establishing of God's pure religion again amongst us, but all your natural subjects in general most effectuously do crave

at your hand to see you entered into the blessed state of wedlock, whereby your Highness' establishment and their [the subjects] assurance might be fully concluded: the hollow-hearted subject feedeth his hope only in this delay.

The Correspondence of Matthew Parker, ed. J. Bruce (London, 1853), p. 131.

Elizabeth Responds to the Pressure to Marry

Throughout her reign, Elizabeth spoke publicly and privately about marriage, but her messages were mixed. In the following excerpts, she offers three reasons for staying single. In the first, she tells Parliament she is already married to England. In the second, she promises to marry and have children when she finds the right man. And in the third, she says she has no inclination to marry.

In a Speech to Parliament, 1558
I have already joyned my selfe in marriage to an husband, namely the kingdome of England. And behold (said she [Elizabeth, in reference to a previous speech] which I marvaile ye have forgotten,) the pledge of this my wedlocke and mariage with my kingdome, (and therewith, she [Elizabeth, in reference to her action in the previous speech] stretched forth her finger and shewed the ring of gold.)

William Camden, *The History of the Most Renowned And Victorious Princess Elizabeth.* 3rd ed. London: B. Fisher, 1635.

In a Private Conversation with Guzman de Silva, Ambassador from Spain, 1565

If I could appoint such a successor to the Crown as would please me and the country, I would not marry, as it is a thing for which I have never had any inclination. My subjects, however press me so that I cannot help myself or take the other course, which if a very difficult one. There is a strong idea in the world that a woman cannot live unless she is married, or at all events that if she refrains from marriage she does so for some bad reason. . . . But what can we do? We cannot cover everybody's mouth, but must content ourselves with doing our duty and trust in God, for the truth will at last be made manifest. He knows my heart, which is very different from what people think, as you will see some day.

Calendar of State Papers: Spain, I, 409–410.

In a Speech to Members of the House of Lords and House of Commons, 1566

I wyll never breke the worde of a prynce spoken in publyke place, for my honour sake. And therefore I saye ageyn, I wyll marrye assone as I can convenyentlye, [conveniently] yf God take not hym awaye with whom I mynde to marrye, or my self, or els [else] sum othere great lette happen. . . . And I hope to have chylderne, otherwyse I wolde never marrie.

Elizabeth, speech to Parliament, 1566.

The Queen's Progresses

Throughout her reign, Elizabeth understood that her success depended upon the support of the English people. To gain popularity and maintain that support, she made public visits into the country and in London. These visits were called "progresses." In the following document, Spanish ambassador Guzman de Silva and English bishop Godfrey Goodman describe two of Elizabeth's progresses. The first is to Reading, a village a short distance outside London. The second is in London. Both accounts show Elizabeth's love for the people and theirs for her.

Reading

She came by the river as far as Reading, and thence through the country in a carriage, open on all sides, that she might be seen by the people, who flocked all along the roads as far as the Duke of Norfolk's houses where she alighted. She was received everywhere with great acclamations and signs of joy, as is customary in this country; whereat she was extremely pleased and told me so, giving me to understand how beloved she was by her subjects and how highly she esteemed this, together with the fact that they were peaceful and contented whilst her neighbors on all sides are in such trouble. She attributed it all to God's miraculous goodness. She ordered her carriage to be taken sometimes where the crowd seemed thickest and stood up and thanked the people.

Calendar of State Papers: Spanish Elizabeth (London, 1894), II, 50–51.

London

In the year '88 [1588], I did then live at the upper end of the Strand near St. Clement's Church, when suddenly there came a report unto us (it was in December, much about five of the clock at night, very dark) that the Queen was gone to council, and if you will see the Queen you must come quickly. Then we all ran; when the Court gates were set open, and no man did hinder us from coming in. There we came where there was a far greater company than was usually at Lenten sermons; and when we had stayed there an hour and that the yard was full, there being a number of torches, the Queen came out in great state. Then we cried, "God save your Majesty! God save your Majesty!" Then the Queen turned unto us and said, "God bless you all, my good people!" Then we cried again, "God save your Majesty! God save your Majesty!" Then the Queen said again unto us, "You may well have a greater prince, but you shall never have a more loving prince:" and so looking one upon another awhile the Queen departed. This wrought such an impression upon us, for shows and pageants are ever best seen by torchlight, that all the way long we did nothing but talk what an admirable Queen she was, and how we would adventure our lives to do her service.

The Court of King James I, ed. J. S. Brewer (London, 1839), p. 163.

Elizabeth Cultivates the Devotion of Her Servants

Elizabeth needed the loyalty of capable men to advise and help her. She kept the devotion of her favorite servants by creating an atmosphere of uncertainty among them and by allowing them to rival for her affection. In the following document the Venetian ambassador to England describes an incident that illustrates her tactics. One of Elizabeth's most devoted courtiers, Robert Dudley, earl of Leicester, loses the queen's favor after an argument with a visitor. But after he shows the proper expression of utter despair, Elizabeth restores Dudley to his favored status.

It being the custom in England on the day of the Epiphany [January 6 in the Christian church calendar] to name a King, a gentleman was chosen who had lately found favor

Robert Dudley, earl of Leicester, was one of Elizabeth's most trusted courtiers. The queen practiced a number of ploys to ensure the loyalty of her servants.

with Queen Elizabeth, and a game of questions and answers being proposed, as usual amongst merry-makers, he commanded Lord Robert [Dudley] to ask the Queen, who was present, which was the most difficult to erase from the mind, an evil opinion created by a wicked informer, or jealousy? And Lord Robert, being unable to refuse, obeyed. The Queen replied courteously that both things were difficult to get rid of, but that, in her opinion, it was much more difficult to remove jealousy.

The game being ended, Lord Robert, angry with that gentleman for having put this question to the Queen, and assigning perhaps a sense to this proceeding other than jest, sent to threaten him, through the medium of a friend, that he would castigate him with a stick. The gentleman replied that this was not punishment for equals, and that if Lord Robert came to insult him, he would find whether his sword cut and thrust, and that if Lord Robert had no quarrel with him Lord Robert was to let him know where he was to be found, because he would then go to Lord Robert quite alone; but the only answer Lord Robert gave was that this gentleman was not his equal, and that he would postpone chastising him till he thought it time to do so.

Shortly afterwards the gentleman went to the Queen, and let her know the whole circumstance. Her Majesty was very angry with Lord Robert, and said that if by her favor he had become insolent he should soon reform, and that she would lower him just as she had at first raised him; and

she banished from the Court the gentleman who had taken his message. Lord Robert was quite confused by the Queen's anger, and, placing himself in one of the rooms of the palace in deep melancholy, remained there four consecutive days, and showing by his despair that he could no longer live; so the Queen, moved to pity, restored him again to her favor; yet, as the Ambassador told me, his [Lord Robert's] good fortune, if perhaps not impeded, will at least have been delayed a little, for it had been said that she would shortly proclaim him Duke and marry him.

Venetian Ambassador, "Leicester." *Calendar of State Papers: Venetian* (London, 1890), VII, 374–375.

The Queen Addresses an Impudent Ambassador

Queen Elizabeth gained respect and power as a leader because she had the knowledge, skills, and wit to solve political and social problems effectively. In the following document, her close adviser Robert Cecil describes a scene involving the queen and the Polish ambassador. The ambassador suggests that the queen has been inattentive in the relations between Poland and England, an issue the queen believes is inappropriate for their meeting. Elizabeth answers the ambassador in fluent Latin, clearly reminding him of his improper behavior, but doing so with diplomacy.

There arrived three days since in the city [London] an ambassador out of Poland, a gentleman of excellent fashion, wit, discourse, language, and person; the Queen was possessed by some of our new counsellors, that are as cunning in intelligence as in deciphering, that his negotiation tendeth to a proposition of peace. Her Majesty, in respect that his father the Duke of Finland had so much honored her, besides the liking she had of this gentleman's comeliness and qualities, brought to her by report, did resolve to receive him publicly, in the chamber of presence, where most of the earls and noblemen about the Court attended, and made it a great day. He was brought in attired in a long robe of black velvet, well jewelled and buttoned, and came to kiss her Majesty's hands where she stood under the state, from whence he straight returned ten yards off, and then began his oration aloud in Latin, with such a gallant countenance, as in my life I never beheld. The effect of it was this, that the King hath sent him to put her Majesty in mind of the ancient confederacies between the Kings of Poland and England; that never a monarch in Europe did willingly neglect their friendship, that he had ever friendly received her merchants and subjects of all quality, that she had suffered his to be spoiled without restitution, not for lack of knowledge of the violences, but out of mere injustice, not caring to minister remedy, notwithstanding many particular petitions and letters received, and to confirm her disposition to avow these courses. . . .

To this I swear by the living God, her Majesty made one of the best answers extempore [without preparation], in Latin, that ever I heard, being much moved to be so challenged in public, especially against her expectation. The words of her beginning were these: " . . . Is this the business your King has sent you about? Surely I can hardly believe, that if the King himself were present, he would have used such language, for if he should, I must have thought that his being a King of not many years, and that not of blood but elected, indeed, newly elected, may leave him uninformed of that course which his father and ancestors have taken with us, and which, peradventure, shall be observed by those that shall come to live after him. And as for you," saieth she to the Ambassador, "although I perceive you have read many books, to fortify your arguments in this case yet I am apt to believe that you have not lighted upon the chapter that prescribeth the form to be used between kings and princes; but were it not for the place you hold, to have so publicly an imputation thrown upon our justice, which as yet never failed, we would answer this audacity of yours in another style; and for the particulars of your negotiations, we will appoint some of our Council to confer with you, to see upon what ground this clamor of yours hath his foundation, who showed yourself rather an herald than an ambassador."

I assure your Lordship, though I am not apt to wonder, I must confess before the living Lord that I never heard her (when I knew her spirits were in a passion) speak with better moderation in my life.

Robert Cecil, "Robert Cecil to the Earl of Essex," in *Queen Elizabeth and Her Times,* ed. Thomas Wright (London, 1838), 478–480.

Elizabeth Sits for a Portrait

Elizabeth was very concerned about her appearance; she felt attractiveness enhanced her power. When she sat for a portrait she hoped the light would capture her best image. She commissioned artist Nicholas Hilliard to create the detailed drawing. In the following document, Hilliard explains that the queen wanted a sunlit setting so that the artist would include no unflattering shadows in his drawing.

This [picture] makes me remember the words also and reasoning of her Majesty when first I came in her Highness' presence to draw, who after showing me how she noted great difference of shadowing in the works and diversity of drawers of sundry [various] nations, and that the Italians [who] had the name to be the cunningest and to draw best, shadowed not, requiring of me the reason of it, seeing that best to show one-self needeth no shadow of place but rather the open light; to which I granted [and] affirmed that shadows in pictures were indeed caused by the shadow of the place or coming in of the light as only one way into the place at some small or high window, which many workmen covet to work in for ease to their sight, and to give unto them a grosser line and a more apparent line to be discerned and maketh the work emboss well, and show very well afar off, which to limning [drawn in sharp detail] work needeth not, because it is to be viewed of necessity in hand near unto the eye. Here her Majesty conceived the reason, and therefore chose her place to sit in for that purpose in the open alley of a goodly garden, where no tree was near, nor any shadow at all, save that as the heaven is lighter than the earth so must that little shadow that was from the earth. This her Majesty's curious demand hath greatly bettered my judgment, besides divers [various] other like questions in art by her most excellent Majesty, which to speak or write of were fitter for some better clerk.

A Treatise Concerning the Arte of Limning, ed. P. Norman (Oxford, 1911–12), I, 28–29.

A Love Letter

The love letter, written to the queen or to an adviser who might conveniently place it where the queen would see it, was a popular way for courtiers to show their admiration for Elizabeth. In July 1592 seafarer and writer Sir Walter Raleigh sent this letter to Robert Cecil, one of Elizabeth's closest advisers. In this document, Raleigh bemoans his separation from the queen.

My heart was never broken till this day that I hear the Queen goes so far off, whom I have followed so many years with so great love and desire in so many journeys, and am now left behind here in a dark prison all alone. While she was yet near at hand that I might hear of her once in two or three days, my sorrows were the less, but even now my heart is cast into the depth of all misery. I

Sir Walter Raleigh was one of the most adventurous explorers of the sixteenth century. His exploits in England and abroad brought him in and out of Elizabeth's favor.

that was wont to behold her riding like Alexander, hunting like Diana, walking like Venus, the gentle wind blowing her fair hair about her pure cheeks like a nymph, sometime sitting in the shade like a goddess, sometime singing like an angel, sometime playing like Orpheus; behold the sorrow of

this world once amiss hath bereaved me of all. Oh! love that only shineth in misfortune, what is become of thy assurance! All wounds have scars but that of phantasy: all affections their relenting but that of woman kind. Who is the judge of friendship but adversity, or when is grace witnessed but in offenses? There were no divinity but by reason of compassion, for revenges are brutish and mortal. All those times past, the loves, the sighs, the sorrows, the desires, can they not weigh down our frail misfortune, cannot one drop of gall [bitterness] be hidden in so great heaps of sweetness? I may then conclude, *spes et fortuna, valete* [hope and fortune, farewell]. She is gone in whom I trusted and of me hath not one thought of mercy nor any respect of that that was. Do with me now therefore what you list [the Queen wishes]. I am more weary of life than they [those more favored] are desirous I should perish, which if it [his perishing] had been for her, as it is by her, had been too happily born.

Sir Walter Raleigh, "Raleigh to Robert Cecil, July, 1592," in *Calendar of the Manuscripts of the Marquis of Salisbury at Hatfield House* (London, 1892), IV, 220.

"Most Gracious Sovereign"

Queen Elizabeth generously praised others and graciously accepted flattery from her admirers. One admirer, poet Sir Philip Sidney, wrote this poem, entitled "Most Gracious Sovereign," to entertain and flatter the queen.

Most Gracious Sovereign

To one whose state is raised over all,
Whose face doth oft [often] the bravest
  sort enchant,
Whose mind is such, as wisest minds
  appall [make pale by comparison],
Who in one self these diverse gifts can plant;
  How dare I (wretch) seek there my
    woes to rest,
  Where ears be burnt, eyes dazzled, heart
    oppres'd?

Your state is great, your greatness is your
  shield,
Your face hurts oft, but still it doth
  delight,
Your mind is wise, your wisdom makes
  you mild;
Such planted gifts enrich ev'n beggars'
  sight.
  So dare I (wretch) my bashful fear subdue,
  And feed mine eyes, mine ears, my heart
    on you.

Sir Philip Sidney, Selected Prose and Poetry. Philip Sidney,
"Most Gracious Sovereign," 1578.

In Praise of Queen Elizabeth's Mind

*Queen Elizabeth inspired many writers to
compose tributes to her. Playwright and prose
writer John Lyly created this piece praising
Elizabeth's intellect, wit, and good gover-
nance.*

Her godly zeal to learning, with her great
skill, hath been so manifestly approved that
I cannot tell whether she deserve more
honor for her knowledge, or admiration for
her courtesy, who in great pomp hath twice
directed her progress [visits] unto the universities, with no less joy to the students than
glory to her state. Here, after long and
solemn disputations in law, physic, and
divinity, not as one wearied with scholars's
arguments, but wedded to their orations,
when every one feared to offend in length,
she in her own person, with no less praise to
her Majesty than delight to her subjects, with
a wise and learned conclusion, both gave
them thanks, and put herself to pains. O
noble pattern of a princely mind, not like to
the kings of Persia, who in their progresses
did nothing else but cut sticks to drive away
the time, nor like the delicate lives of the
Sybarites [Inhabitants of the ancient city of
Sybaris in southern Italy. They were noted
for their luxury.], who would not admit any
art to be exercised within their city that
might make the least noise. Her wit so sharp,
that if I should repeat the apt answers, the
subtle questions, the fine speeches, the pithy
sentences, which on the sudden she hath
uttered, they would rather breed admiration
than credit. But such are the gifts that the living God hath indued [given] her withal, that
look in what art or language, wit or learning,
virtue or beauty any one hath particularly
excelled most, she only hath generally
exceeded every one in all, insomuch that
there is nothing to be added that either man
would wish in a woman, or God doth give
to a creature. . . .

But all these graces, although they be to
be wondered at, yet her politic government,

her prudent counsel, her zeal to religion, her clemency to those that submit, her stoutness to those that threaten, so far exceed all other virtues that they are more easy to be marveled at than imitated.

John Lyly, "On Queen Elizabeth," From *Euphues and His England, 1580.*

The Perfect Courtier

Courtiers at the queen's court were attractive young men expected to behave properly. They were to be jovial and entertaining gentlemen with sweet natures. The handbook for Elizabethan courtiers, entitled The Courtier, *was written by an Italian named Baldassare Castiglione in Urbino, Italy, in 1528 and translated into English by Thomas Hoby in 1561. This excerpt from Castiglione's book*

describes a conversation among a count and several lords identifying a courtier's most important qualities.

Then answered the Count: . . . "I will have this our courtier therefore to be a gentleman born and of a good house. For it is a great deal less dispraise [embarrassing] for him that is not born a gentleman to fail in the acts of virtue than for a gentleman. If he swerve from the steps his of ancestors, he staineth the name of his family. . . . The noble of birth count it a shame not to arrive at the least at the bounds of their predecessors set forth unto them. . . . Some there are born indued [given] with such graces that they seem not to have been born but rather fashioned with the very hand of some god, and abound in all goodness both of body and mind. . . .

Elizabeth's courtiers were expected to behave like gentlemen and to dress in the fashion of the day. Here, a sculpture depicts the sumptuous dress of the queen and her court.

"Likewise in company with men and women of all degrees, in sporting, in laughing, and in jesting, he hath in him certain sweetness, and so comely demeanors, that who so speaketh with him, or yet beholdeth him, must needs bear him an affection forever. . . .

"And to avoid envy and to keep company pleasantly with every man, let him do whatsoever other men do, so he decline not at any time from commendable deeds, but governeth himself with that good judgment that will not suffer him to enter into any folly. But let him laugh, dally, jest, and dance yet in such wise [ways] that he may always declare himself to be witty and discreet and everything that he doth or speaketh, let him do it with a grace."

Then answered the Lord Cesar: . . . "If I do well bear in mind, me think, Count Lewis, you have this night oftentimes repeated that the courtier ought to accompany all his doings, gestures, demeanors, finally all his motions with a grace. And this, me think, ye put for a sauce [topping] to everything, without the which his other properties and good conditions were little worth. . . ."

The Lord Julian answered, "There is no doubt but so excellent and perfect a courtier hath need to understand . . . not only to speak but also to write well."

"Nay, everyone shall understand him," answered the Count, "for fineness hindereth not the easiness of understanding. Neither will I have him to speak always in gravity, but of pleasant matters, of merry conceits, of honest devices, and of jests according to the time. . . . And when he shall then commune of a matter that is dark

and hard, I will have him, both in words and sentences well pointed, to express his judgment, and to make every doubt clear and plain after a certain diligent sort without tediousness. . . ."

The Lord Octavian said: "I think . . . that the courtier, if he be of the perfection that Count Lewis and Sir Frederick have described him, may indeed be a good thing and worthy praise, but for all that not simply, nor of himself but for respect of that whereto he may be applied. . . .

"But I would say rather that many of the qualities appointed him—as dancing, singing, and sporting—were lightness and vanity, and in a man of estimation rather to be dispraised than commended. . . .

"The end therefore of a perfect courtier, whereof hitherto nothing hath been spoken, I believe is to purchase him, by the means of the qualities which these lords have given him, in such wise the goodwill and favor of the prince he is in service withal. . . .

"And, therefore, in mine opinion, as music, sports, pastimes, and other pleasant fashions are, as a man would say, the flower of courtliness, even so is the training and helping forward of the prince to goodness, and the fearing him from evil, the fruit of it."

Baldassare Castiglione, *The Book of the Courtier*, trans. Sir Thomas Hoby, 1928.

A Courtier's Companions and Apparel

In 1529 a Spanish priest named Don Antonio de Guevara wrote a guidebook that

Lord Chancellor Christopher Hatton sits for a portrait in elegant dress.

told courtiers how they should look and act. In 1557 writer Sir Thomas North translated it into English and gave it the title The Diall of Princes. *In the following excerpt, Guevara recommends that courtiers keep good company and wear fine and stylish clothing.*

The wise courtier, both in court and out of court, and in all places where he cometh, must take great regard he accompany with none but with wise and virtuous men. For if he do not, he cannot win nor acquire such honor by his well doing, as he shall lose his credit by keeping ill company. And therefore he shall enforce himself always to be in the presence and company of virtuous and noble men, and shall confer with the most grave, wise, and honest gentlemen of the court. For using this way, he shall bind them to him, by reason of his daily access to them. . . .

These young gentlemen courtiers must take heed that they become not troublesome, importunate, nor quarrellers, that they be not filchers [thieves], liars, vagabonds, and slanderers, nor any way given to vice. As for other things, I would not seem to take from them their pastime and pleasure but that they may use them at their own pleasure. And in all other things lawful and irreprovable, observing time and hours convenient, and therewithal to accompany themselves with their fellows and companions.

Also the young courtier that cometh newly to the court must of necessity be very well apparelled, according to his degree and calling, and his servants that follow him well appointed. For in court men regard not only the house and family he cometh of, but mark also his apparel and servants that follow him. And I mislike one thing very much, that about the court they do rather honor and reverence a man brave and sumptuous in apparel being vicious, than they do a man that is grave, wise, and virtuous. And yet nevertheless the courtier may assure himself of this, that few will esteem of him, either for that he is virtuous or nobly born, if he be not also sumptuously apparelled and well accompanied, for then only will every man account and esteem of him. . . .

Albeit the courtier come of a noble house, and that he be young of years, rich, and wealthy, yet would I like better he

21

should use rather a certain mean and measure in his apparel (wearing that that is comely and gentlemanlike) than others of most cost and worship. For like as they would count him a fool for wearing that he could not pay for, so they likewise would think him simple, if he wear not that that become him, and that he might easily come by. His apparel should be agreeable with his years, that is to say, on the holy days some more richer and braver than on the work days, and in the winter of the hottest furs, in the summer light garments of satin and damask, and to ride [horses] with some others of lesser price and more durable. For as the wisdom of man is known by his speaking, so is his discretion discerned by his apparel.

Don Antonio de Guevara, "What Company the Courtier Should Keep and How He Should Apparel Himself." From *The Diall of Princes*, trans. Sir Thomas North, 1557. In *English Literature and Its Backgrounds.*

Petty Squabbles at Court

At Elizabeth's court, disagreements and fighting often broke out among courtiers. This document illustrates how the courtiers Sussex and North began fighting because North agreed with the queen that Sussex had provided too few dishes at a feast.

This Queen has greatly feasted Alençon's [the French duke of Anjou] ambassador, and on one occasion when she was entertaining him at dinner she thought the sideboard [buffet] was not so well furnished with pieces of plate [assortments of food]

as she would like the Frenchman to have seen it; she therefore called the Earl of Sussex, the Lord Steward, who had charge of these things, and asked him how it was there was so little plate. The Earl replied that he had, for many years, accompanied her and other sovereigns of England in their progresses, and he had never seen them take so much plate as she was carrying then. The Queen told him to hold his tongue, that he was a great rogue, and that the more good that was done to people like him the worse they got. She then turned to a certain North [a courtier], who was there in the room, and asked him whether he thought there was much or little plate on the sideboard, to which he replied there was very little, and threw the blame on Sussex. When North left the Queen's chamber, Sussex told him that he had spoken wrongly and falsely in what he said to the Queen, whereupon North replied that if he, Sussex, did not belong to the Council he would prove what he said to his teeth. Sussex then went to [Robert Dudley, earl of] Leicester and complained of the knavish behavior of North but Leicester told him that the words he used should not be applied to such persons as North. Sussex answered that, whatever he might think of the words, North was a great knave, so that they remained offended with one another as they had been before on other matters. This may not be of importance, but I have thought well to relate it so that you may see how easily matters here may now be brought into discord if care be not taken on one side to insure support against eventualities [situations that might come up].

"The Queen at Court." In *Elizabeth I*. Ed. Joseph M. Levine. Englewood Cliffs, NJ: Prentice-Hall, 1969. Reprint August 14, 1578. From *Calendar of State Papers: Spanish Elizabeth* (London, 1894), 606–607.

Elizabeth's Last Days

In the following excerpt, courtier Robert Carey describes Queen Elizabeth's last days. She died in the early morning hours of March 24, 1603.

When I came to court, I found the Queen ill disposed and she kept her inner lodging; yet she, hearing of my arrival, sent for me. I found her in one of her withdrawing chambers, sitting low upon her cushions. She called me to her; I kissed her hand, and told her it was my chiefest happiness to see her in safety, and in health, which I wished might long continue. She took me by the hand, and wrung it hard, and said, "No, Robin [Robert], I am not well," and then discoursed with me of her indisposition [illness], and that her heart had been sad and heavy for ten or twelve

The effigy from the tomb of Queen Elizabeth in Westminster Abbey. The people of London responded to news of her death with tremendous sorrow.

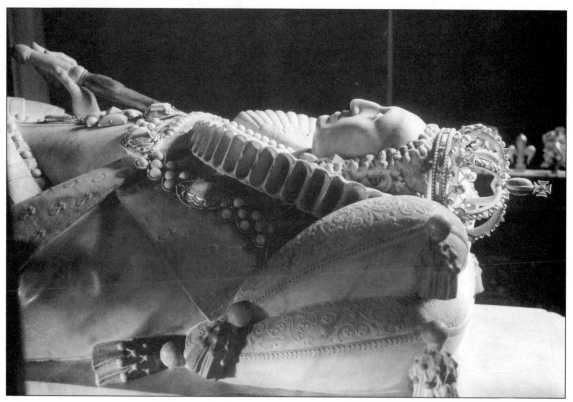

days; and in her discourse, she fetched not so few as forty or fifty great sighs. I was grieved at the first to see her in this plight; for in all my lifetime before, I never knew her fetch a sigh, but when [her sister, Mary] the Queen of Scots was beheaded. . . .

I used the best words I could, to persuade her from this melancholy humor; but I found by her it was too deep-rooted in her heart, and hardly to be removed. This was upon a Saturday night, and she gave command, that the great closet [large bedroom] should be prepared for her to go to chapel the next morning. The next day, all things being in a readiness, we long expected her coming. After eleven o'clock, one of the grooms came out, and bade make ready for the private closet [small bedroom], she would not go to the great. There we stayed long for her coming, but at the last she had cushions laid for her in the privy chamber hard by the closet door, and there she heard service.

From that day forwards, she grew worse and worse. She remained upon her cushions four days and nights at the least. All about her could not persuade her, either to take any sustenance, or go to bed. . . .

The Queen grew worse and worse, because she would be so, none about her being able to persuade her to go to bed. My Lord Admiral was sent for (who, by reason of my sister's death, that was his wife, had absented himself some fortnight from court). What by fair means, what by force, he got her to bed. There was no hope of her recovery, because she refused all remedies.

On Wednesday, the 23rd of March [1603], she grew speechless. That afternoon, by signs, she called for her council, and by putting her hand to her head, when the King of Scots was named to succeed her, they all knew he was the man she desired should reign after her.

About six at night she made signs for the Archbishop and her chaplains to come to her, at which time I went in with them, and sat upon my knees full of tears to see that heavy sight. Her Majesty lay upon her back, with one hand in the bed, and the other without. The Bishop kneeled down by her, and examined her first of her faith; and she so punctually answered all his several questions, by lifting up her eyes, and holding up her hand, as it was a comfort to all the beholders. Then the good man told her plainly what she was, and what she was to come to; and though she had been long a great Queen here upon earth, yet shortly she was to yield an account of her stewardship to the King of Kings. After this he began to pray, and all that were by did answer him. After he had continued long in prayer, till the old man's knees were weary, he blessed her, and meant to rise and leave her. The Queen made a sign with her hand. My sister, Lady Scroop, knowing her meaning, told the Bishop the Queen desired he would pray still. He did so for a long half hour after, and then thought to leave her. The second time she made sign to have him continue in prayer. He did so for half an hour more, with earnest cries to God for her soul's health, which he uttered with that fervency of spirit, as the Queen, to all our sight, much rejoiced thereat, and gave testimony, to us all of her Christian and comfortable end. By this time it grew late, and every one departed, all but her women that attended her. . . .

I went to my lodging, and left word with one in the cofferer's [treasurer's] chamber to call me, if that night it was thought she would die, and gave the porter an angel [messenger] to let me in at any time when I called. Between one and two of the clock on Thursday morning, he that I left in the cofferer's chamber, brought me word the Queen was dead. . . .

Robert Carey, "Robert Carey Describes the Queen's Last Days." In *Memoirs of the Life of Robert Carey* (London, 1759), pp. 115–123.

London Reacts to the Queen's Death

In the following excerpt, diarist John Manningham describes the events in London and the sorrow of the English people immediately following Elizabeth's death.

This morning [March 24, 1603] about three at clock her Majesty departed this life, mildly like a lamb, easily like a ripe apple from the tree. . . . Dr. Parry [the Queen's doctor] told me that he was present, and sent his prayers before her soul; and I doubt not but she is amongst the royal saints in Heaven in eternal joys.

About ten at clock the Counsel and divers [various] noblemen having been a while in consultation, proclaimed James VI, King of Scots, the King of England, France, and Ireland, beginning at Whitehall [Palace] gates; where Sir Robert Cecil read the proclamation which he carried in his hand, and after read again in Cheapside [a suburb of London]. Many noblemen, lords spiritual and temporal [secular], knights, five trumpets, many heralds. The gates at Ludgate and portcullis [gates of the city] were shut and down, by the Lord Mayor's command, who was there present, with the Aldermen, etc., and until he had a token beside promise . . . that they would proclaim the King of Scots King of England, he would not open.

Upon the death of a King or Queen in England the Lord Mayor of London is the greatest magistrate in England. All corporations and their governors continue, most of the other officers' authority is expired with the prince's [monarch's] breath. There was a diligent watch and ward kept at every gate and street, day and night, by householders, to prevent garboils [uproar]: which God be thanked were more feared than perceived.

The proclamation was heard with great expectation and silent joy, no great shouting. I think the sorrow for her Majesty's departure was so deep in many hearts they could not so suddenly show any great joy, though it could not be less than exceeding great for the succession of so worthy a king. And at night they showed it by bonfires and ringing. No tumult, no contradiction, no disorder in the city; every man

This elegant portrait of a young Elizabeth captures the beauty and grace of the queen beloved by her courtiers and subjects.

went about his business, as readily, as peaceably, as securely, as though there had been no change, nor any news ever heard of competitors. God be thanked, our King hath his right!

The Diary of John Manningham, ed. John Bruce (London, 1868), pp. 146–147.

"Epitaph on Elizabeth"

In 1616 playwright and poet Ben Jonson wrote this short poem in honor of Queen Elizabeth. In the poem, Jonson proclaims her beauty and virtue and says that if she had faults, they should remain buried with her.

Would'st thou hear what man can say
In a little? Reader, stay.

Underneath this stone doth lie
As much beauty as could die:
Which in life did harbor give
To more virtue than doth live.

If at all she had a fault,
Leave it buried in this vault.
One name was Elizabeth,
The other, let it sleep with death!
Fitter, where it died, to tell,
Than that it lived at all. Farewell!

Ben Jonson, "Epitaph on Elizabeth L.H," 1616.

Political and Social Issues

R uling England during the sixteenth century was not easy. Elizabeth faced many political and social issues that threatened her reign. She had to address these issues and resolve them diplomatically in order to maintain the support of the English people and prevent foreign countries from invading England.

Elizabeth's most pressing problem was the threat of war with foreign powers, especially other European nations. England was strong militarily during this time, but it was by no means the most powerful country in Europe. France, Spain, Holland, and others also vied for that title. To prevent one nation from becoming too powerful, the nations of Europe formed alliances, agreements between countries to protect one another in case of attack. France, for example, made an alliance with Scotland. Elizabeth, in turn, allied herself with Spain. When English ships began raiding Spanish vessels at sea, that alliance fell apart, however, and Elizabeth formed a relationship with Holland and France. This system of alliances maintained a balance of power in Europe and prevented one country from overrunning the others.

Religion was another troubling issue. At the time, there were two dominant forms of Christianity in Europe: Catholicism and Protestantism. The belief systems of these two religions differed greatly on issues such as the number of holy sacraments (special religious rites), the Catholic requirement that parishioners make monetary donations to their church or complete a series of good works to get into heaven, and the Protestant belief that people could have a personal relationship with God. There was also a general sense from the Protestants that the Catholic church was corrupt. Before Elizabeth even came to power, Protestants in England ousted the Catholic Church, which had once been the country's official church, and installed Protestantism in its place. When Elizabeth took the throne, she, a Protestant, wanted to make sure that her religion remained dominant in England.

Although she faced dissent from Catholics inside and outside the country, Elizabeth

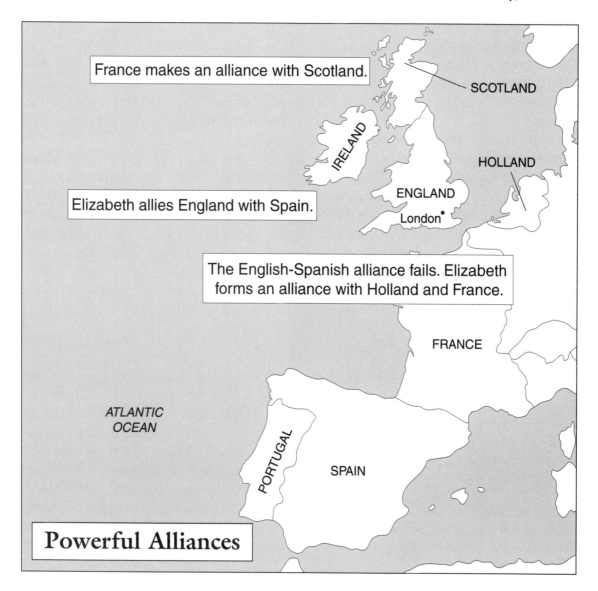

France makes an alliance with Scotland.

SCOTLAND

IRELAND

HOLLAND

ENGLAND

London

Elizabeth allies England with Spain.

The English-Spanish alliance fails. Elizabeth forms an alliance with Holland and France.

FRANCE

ATLANTIC OCEAN

PORTUGAL

SPAIN

Powerful Alliances

took measures to ensure that the Protestant Church of England remained the state church. One way she did this was to declare that all worshipers use the Protestant *Book of Common Prayer* during worship services. The *Book of Common Prayer* established a standard order of worship. Another way she encouraged Protestantism was to pass laws requiring all English subjects to attend Protestant churches. Although Elizabeth did not require Catholics in England officially to renounce their religious beliefs, she did demand that they not attend Catholic churches.

This debate over religion caused Elizabeth some problems. In particular, outside forces threatened her position as queen. Some foreign Catholics, among them Elizabeth's cousin Mary, Queen of Scots, wanted to depose Elizabeth by any means necessary and return Catholicism to England. Mary and several accomplices spent many years plotting to overthrow and even assassinate Elizabeth in an effort to accomplish this. However, Elizabeth was a strong and able ruler who refused to fall prey to such conspiracies. In 1587, she had Mary executed.

Social problems were also a concern. As England's population increased, for example, so did the number of people living in poverty. The government itself was unable to support so many poor, so in the early 1560s, Elizabeth and Parliament, England's legislative body, passed a series of laws that required people with money to donate a fixed amount monthly to help the poor. Those who refused faced criminal prosecution.

During her forty-five-year reign, Elizabeth managed her country's problems with a style that proved successful. She maintained peace in England, preserved the Church of England, and ensured domestic order. The documents in this chapter explain the queen's political power and how she worked with Parliament to ensure political and social success in England.

The Powers of Parliament

Parliament, England's legislative body, consists of two houses: the House of Lords, made up of noblemen, and the House of Commons, made up of elected members. During Elizabeth's time, Parliament passed laws, levied taxes, and granted social rights and status to individuals. In the following document, historian William Camden outlines some of the powers of the English Parliament.

The most high and absolute power of the realm of England consisteth in the Parliament . . . The Parliament abrogateth [abolishes] old laws, maketh new, giveth order for things past and for things hereafter to be followed, changeth rights and possessions of private men, legitimateth bastards, establisheth forms of religion, altereth weights and measures, giveth forms of succession to the crown, defineth of doubtful rights whereof is no law already made, appointeth subsidies, tailles [royal tax on nonprivileged subjects], taxes and impositions, giveth most free pardons and absolutions, restoreth in blood and name, as the highest court, condemneth or absolveth them whom the prince [king or queen] will put to that trial. And to be short, all that ever the people of [ancient] Rome might do, either in *centuriatis comitiis* or *tributis* [an assembly of the people or of the tribes], the same may be done by the Parliament of England, which representeth and hath the power of the whole realm, both the head and the body. For every Englishman is intended to be there present, either in person or by procuration [having an authorized representative] and attorney, . . . from the prince (be he king or queen) to the lowest person of England. And the consent of the parliament is taken to be every man's consent.

The Speaker [the Leader of Parliament] . . . is commonly appointed by the king or queen, though accepted by the assent of the House.

No bill is an Act of Parliament . . . until both the houses [the House of Commons and the House of Lords] severally have agreed unto it . . . no, nor then neither. But the last day of that parliament or session the prince cometh in person in his parliament robes, and sitteth in his state . . . Then one reads the titles of every Act which hath passed at that session . . . : it is marked there what the prince doth allow, and to such he saith [in Latin], *Le Roy* or *La Royne le veult* . . . To those which the prince liketh not, *Le Roy* or *La Royne s'ad-*visera, and those be accounted utterly dashed and of none effect . . .

William Camden, "Of the Parliament and the Authority Thereof." *Select Statutes and Other Constitutional Documents Illustrative of the Reigns of Elizabeth and James I.* G.W. Prothero, ed. 4th ed. London: Oxford University Press, 1913. Reprint from *The Commonwealth of England*, ed. 1589, Bk. II. Chaps. 2–4.

The Powers of the Queen

According to the English constitution, the monarch had absolute power over all matters in England. In the following document, historian William Camden describes some of those powers, including the right to declare war, the right to choose advisers and law enforcement officers, the power to punish individuals, the control over state spending, and the right to issue proclamations.

The Prince [the king or queen] . . . hath absolutely in his power the authority of war, and peace . . . His privy council [advisers] be chosen also at the prince's pleasure . . . In war time and in the field the prince hath also absolute power . . . : he may put to death or to other bodily punishment whom he shall think so to deserve, without process of law or form of judgment. This hath been sometime used within the realm before any open war, in sudden insurrections and rebellions, but that not allowed of wise and grave men . . . This absolute power is called martial law . . . The prince useth also absolute power in crying and decreeing the money of the realm by his proclamation only . . . The prince useth

Although Elizabeth regularly conferred with her courtiers, the monarch wielded absolute power over all matters of government.

those that hold land of him in chief . . . To be short, the prince is the life, the head and the authority of all things that be done in the realm of England.

William Camden, "Of the Monarch, King or Queen of England." *Select Statutes and Other Constitutional Documents Illustrative of the Reigns of Elizabeth and James I.* G.W. Prothero, ed. 4th ed. London: Oxford University Press, 1913. Reprint from *The Commonwealth of England*, ed. 1589, Bk. II. Chaps. 2–4.

Recruiting Horsemen for the Military

Parliament recruited soldiers with weapons, armor, and horses to fight in the army. This document, a 1569 letter sent to knights and local officials, provides details for equipment and pay and gives the time and location where recruited soldiers should assemble.

Forasmuch as we [Parliament] have by advice of our council resolved and accorded to direct our letters under our signet [signature] being in your [the queen's] custody to sundry [various] knights, esquires and others of ability in diverse shires of our realm, for to command them to put in order and furniture certain horsemen . . . as more at large may appear by the tenour of our said letters, the copy whereof . . . hereafter also followeth. . . .

Trusty and well beloved, we greet you well. Forasmuch as we have necessary occasion to levy certain numbers of horsemen to serve us in the north parts of our realm, as well for demi-lances [small swords] as for light horsemen, wherein we are to require,

also to dispense with laws made, whereas equity requireth a moderation to be had, and with pains for transgression of laws . . . The prince giveth all the chief and highest offices or magistracies of the realm . . . All writs, executions and commandments be done in the prince's name . . . The prince hath the wardship and first marriage of all as reason is, the aid of our good and faithful subjects in sundry shires of our realm; having well considered the ability of such persons as do remain or have their possessions in that shire, meet for that purpose, with assurance also of their good wills to serve us and our crown, we have made choice of you, and require and therewith also charge you that with all speed possible you put in a readiness one able man and a horse or able gelding fully furnished with armour, weapon and all other things requisite to serve in the wars as a demilance or light horseman; and the same to send away in company with others in that shire in such sort as, accounting the distance of the place from whence he shall depart, he may be in good and serviceable sort at our city of York before the first or fourth day of April next [1569]; and there shall be paid unto him money for his coat [uniform] and conduct [service]. And we assure you that the horse and armour, after service done, shall be safely returned unto you, if in service the same perish not, or that the fault be not in the horseman himself. And for further instruction how you shall arm and apparel the said horseman, you shall receive knowledge of our lieutenant in that county, or of such others that have charge there for that purpose, whose directions we require you to follow.

Given under our signet at our Honour of Hampton Court, the 10th day of March, 1569.

Quoted in G.W. Prothero, ed., *Select Statutes and Other Constitutional Documents Illustrative of the Reigns of Elizabeth and James I.* 4th ed. London: Oxford University Press, 1913. Reprint from *Burleigh Papers*, I. p. 578.

Elizabeth Defines Her Role as Queen

From the beginning of her reign, Elizabeth wanted England to be a peaceful and prosperous nation. In the first excerpt below, a speech before Parliament in 1593, Elizabeth confirms that her goal has been not to enlarge English territory, as some might expect of a monarch, but to reign well over the England she inherited. In the second excerpt, a speech before Parliament in 1601, she sums up her purpose as a monarch: serving God and defending England from peril.

It may be thought simplicity in me that all this time of my reign I have not sought to advance my territories and enlarge my dominions, for opportunity hath served me to do it. I acknowledge my womanhood and weakness in that respect. But it hath not been the hardness to obtain, or doubt how to keep the things so obtained, that only hath withheld me from these attempts. My mind was never to invade my neighbors, or to usurp over any. I am contented to reign over mine own and to rule as a just prince. . . .

To be a King and wear a crown is a thing more glorious to them that see it, than it is pleasant to them that bear it. For myself, I was never so enticed with the glorious name of a King or royal authority of a Queen, as delighted that God hath made me His instrument to maintain His truth and glory, and to defend this Kingdom (as

I said) from peril, dishonour, and tyranny and oppression.

Elizabeth I, quoted in *"The Heart and Stomach of a King": Elizabeth and the Politics of Sex and Power.* By Carole Levin. Philadelphia: University of Pennsylvania Press, 1994.

Elizabeth Rallies Her Troops

During the 1580s England's relationship with Spain deteriorated for two reasons. First, British naval ships began raiding Spanish ships. Second, representatives of the Spanish king were trying to restore Catholicism in England. When a plot linked to Spanish king Philip II threatened Elizabeth's life, war between England and Spain became inevitable. In the ensuing battle, called the Battle of the Spanish Armada, the British navy soundly defeated the Spanish navy. This 1588 victory established British supremacy at sea. On the eve of the war with Spain, Elizabeth visited her troops dressed as a soldier. She spoke to inspire them for the upcoming battle; her speech is excerpted here.

My Loving People: We have been persuaded by some that are careful of our safety, to take heed how we commit ourselves to armed multitudes, for fear of treachery; but I assure you, I do not desire to live to distrust my faithful and loving people.

Let tyrants fear; I have always so behaved myself, that, under God, I have placed my chiefest strength and safeguard in the loyal hearts and good will of my subjects, and therefore, I am come amongst you, as you see, at this time, not for my recreation and disport [entertainment], but being resolved in the midst and heat of the battle, to live or die amongst you all, to lay down for my God, and for my kingdoms, and for my people, my honor and my blood, even in the dust.

Queen Elizabeth visits her troops on the eve of the Battle of the Spanish Armada.

I know I have the body but of a weak and feeble woman; but I have the heart and stomach of a king, and of a king of England too; and think foul scorn that Parma or Spain, or any prince of Europe should dare to invade the borders of my realm; to which rather than any dishonor shall grow by me, I myself will take up arms, I myself will be your general, judge, and rewarder of every one of your virtues in the field.

I know already, for your forwardness you have deserved rewards and crowns; and we do assure you in the word of a prince, they shall be duly paid you. In the meantime, my lieutenant-general shall be in my stead, than whom never prince commanded a more noble or worthy subject; not doubting but by your obedience to my general, by your concord in the camp, and your valor in the field, we shall shortly have a famous victory over those enemies of my God, of my kingdoms, and of my people.

Somers Tracts, W. Scoff, ed., (London, 1809), I, 429–430.

Restrictions on Catholics

In 1593 Parliament passed and the queen approved an act which restricted the movement of Catholics who refused to attend Protestant services in the Church of England. During Elizabeth's time, the English government suspected Catholics of conspiring to overthrow the queen. Thus, the 1593 act was aimed at stopping such activity. This document names the crimes against Catholic citizens and priests and identifies the limitations placed on them. They were restricted from travel and punished if they refused to comply.

For the better discovering and avoiding of such traiterous and most dangerous conspiracies and attempts, as are daily devised and practised against our most gracious Sovereign Lady the Queen's Majesty and the happy estate of this Commonweal by sundry [various] wicked and seditious persons, who terming themselves Catholics and being indeed spies and intelligencers [those who compile evidence] not only for her Majesty's foreign enemies but also for rebellious and traiterous subjects born within her Highness' dominions, and hiding their most detestable and devilish purposes under a false pretext of religion and conscience, do secretly wander and shift from place to place within this realm, to corrupt and seduce her Majesty's subjects, and to stir them to sedition and rebellion: Be it enacted . . . That every person above the age of sixteen years, born within any the Queen's Majesty's dominions or made denizen [residents], being a Popish recusant [Catholic] and before the end of this session of Parliament convicted for not repairing [returning] to some church, chapel or usual place of common prayer to hear divine service there . . . and having any certain place of abode within this realm, shall within forty days next after the end of this session of Parliament (if they be within this realm, and not restrained [by various specified hindrances] . . .) repair to their place of dwelling where they usually heretofore made their common abode, and shall not any time after remove above five miles from thence . . . , upon pain that every person that shall offend against the tenor of this Act in anything before-mentioned shall forfeit all his goods and chattels [personal property], and shall also forfeit to the Queen's Majesty all [his] lands [&c.] during the life of the same offender. . . .

And be it further enacted, That if any person which shall be suspected to be a Jesuit [a Catholic order], seminary or massing priest, being examined by any person having lawful authority in that behalf to examine such person which shall be so suspected, shall refuse to answer directly and truly whether he be a Jesuit or [&c.] as is aforesaid, every such person so refusing to answer shall . . . be committed to prison by such as shall examine him . . . and thereupon shall remain in prison without bail or mainprize [warrant of release], until he shall make direct and true answer to the said questions whereupon he shall be so examined . . .

Quoted in G.W. Prothero, ed., *Select Statutes and Other Constitutional Documents Illustrative of the Reigns of Elizabeth and James I.* 4th ed. London: Oxford University Press, 1913. Reprint from *Documents. Reign of Elizabeth. Statute 35 of the Eighth Parliament.*

Elizabeth's Proclamation Against Nonconformists

Keeping England Protestant was very important to Elizabeth and her government. Thus, she made many rulings in support of the Protestant Church of England. One such ruling required that worshipers use a book called the Book of Common Prayer *during church services. Some people who wanted to form different Protestant sects, called Nonconformists, spoke out against this book. Elizabeth remained firm, however, and in the following excerpt, she commands that her subjects use the* Book of Common Prayer.

The Queen's Majesty being right sorry to understand that the order [Book] of Common Prayer set forth by the common consent of the realm and by authority of parliament in the first year of her reign [1559], wherein is nothing contained but the scripture of God and that which is consonant [in agreement] unto it, is now of late of some men despised and spoken against, both by open preachings and writings, and of some bold and vain curious men new and other rites found out and frequented; whereupon contentions, sects and disquietness doth arise among her people, and, for one godly and uniform order, diversity of rites and ceremonies, disputations and contentions, schism and divisions already risen, and more like to ensue: the cause of which disorders her Majesty doth plainly understand to be the negligence of the bishops and other magistrates, who should cause the good laws and acts of parliament made in this behalf to be better executed, and not so dissembled and winked at as hitherto it may appear that they have been:

For speedy remedy whereof her Majesty straitly chargeth and commandeth all archbishops and bishops . . . and all other who have any authority, to put in execution the Act for the uniformity of Common Prayer and the administration of the sacraments, made in the first year of her gracious reign, with all diligence and severity . . .

And if any persons shall either in private houses or in public places make assemblies and therein use other rites of Common Prayer and administration of the sacraments than is prescribed in the said book, or shall maintain in their houses any persons being notoriously charged by books or preachings to attempt the alteration of the said orders, they shall see such persons punished with all severity, according to the laws of this realm, by pains appointed in the said Act.

Elizabeth I, "A Proclamation against the Despisers or Breakers of the Orders Prescribed in the Book of Common Prayer." *Select Statutes and Other Constitutional Documents Illustrative of the Reigns of Elizabeth and James I.* G.W. Prothero, ed. 4th ed. London: Oxford University Press, 1913. Reprint from *Cardwell, Documentary Annals*, I. p. 348.

The Queen Promises Freedom of Religious Conviction

Although Elizabeth insisted that England be a Protestant nation, she did not generally mind her subjects being Catholic as long as they followed the laws requiring English citizens to attend weekly Protestant church services. Here, Elizabeth explains that, despite rumors to the contrary, she has no intention of intervening in the religious affairs of subjects who adhere to English law.

Whereas certain rumors are carried and spread abroad among sundry [various] her Majesty's subjects, that her Majesty hath caused, or will hereafter cause, inquisition [investigation] and examination to be had of men's consciences in matters of religion; her Majesty would have it known, that such reports are utterly untrue, and grounded either of malice, or of some fear more than there is cause. For although certain persons have been lately convented [assembled] before her Majesty's council upon just causes, and that some of them have been treated withal upon some matter of religion; yet the cause thereof hath grown merely of themselves; in that they have first manifestly [apparently] broken the laws established for religion, in not coming at all to the church, to common prayer and divine service, as of late time before they were accustomed, and had used by the space of nine or ten whole years altogether: so as if thereby they had not given manifest [obvious] occasion by their open and wilful contempt of breaking of her Majesty's laws, they had not been anything molested, or dealt withal.

Wherefore, her Majesty would have all her loving subjects to understand, that, as long as they shall openly continue in the observation of her laws, and shall not wilfully and manifestly break them by their open actions, her Majesty's meaning is, not to have any of them molested by any inquisition or examination of their consciences in causes of religion; but will accept and entreat them as her good and obedient subjects. And if any shall otherwise by their open deeds and facts declare themselves wilfully disobedient to break her laws; then she cannot but use them according to their deserts [behavior that deserves punishment], and will not forbear [hold back] to inquire to their demeanors, and of what mind and disposition they are, as by her laws her Majesty shall find it necessary.

John Strype, *Annals of the Reformation* (Oxford, 1824). I, ii, 370–371.

An Act Protecting Elizabeth

Throughout her reign, Elizabeth's life and status as queen were threatened by her cousin Mary, Queen of Scots, who wanted to rule England herself, and by religious and foreign powers that wanted to restore Catholicism in England. To protect the queen, Parliament passed several laws in 1581 that made it illegal to speak out against the queen or spread rumors about her. This document explains that anyone caught breaking these laws would suffer harsh penalties, including imprisonment, having one's ears cut off, or execution.

I. Whereas by the laws and statutes of this realm, already made against seditious words and rumours uttered against the Queen's most excellent Majesty, there is not sufficient and condign [adequate] punishment provided for to suppress the malice of such as be evil affected towards her Highness: be it therefore enacted, That if any person . . . shall advisedly and with a malicious intent . . . speak any false, sedi-

tious and slanderous news, rumours, sayings or tales against our said most natural Sovereign Lady the Queen's Majesty that now is, that then every such person, being thereof lawfully convicted or attainted [disgraced] in form hereafter in this present Act expressed, shall for every such first offence either be in some market place within the shire, city or borough where the said words were spoken, set openly upon the pillory [a wooden frame for locking a person's head and hands] . . . if it shall fortune to be without any city or town corporate, and if it shall happen to be within any city or town corporate . . . to have both his ears cut off; or at the election [time of release] of the offender pay £200 [approximately $8,000 in today's values] to the Queen's Highness' use . . . and also shall suffer imprisonment by the space of six months . . .

II. And be it further enacted, That all persons which shall advisedly and with malicious intent against our said Sovereign Lady report any false, seditious and slanderous news, rumours or tales, to the slander and defamation of our said Sovereign Lady the Queen's Majesty that now is, of the speaking or reporting of any other, that then all persons so reporting, being thereof convicted and attainted in form hereafter in this Act expressed, shall for every such first offence either be in some market place within the shire . . . or town where the said words were reported set openly upon the pillory . . . if it shall fortune to be without any city or town corporate, and if it shall happen to be within any city or town corporate . . . to have one of his ears cut off; or at the election of the offender pay 200 marks [approximately $5,300 in today's value] to the Queen's Highness' use . . . , and shall also suffer imprisonment by the space of three months . . .

III. And be it further enacted, That if any person once lawfully convicted for any of the offences aforesaid, do afterwards eftsoones [once again] offend in any of the offences aforesaid, that then every such second offence to be deemed felony, and the offender to suffer such pains of death and forfeiture [execution] as in case of felony, without any benefit of clergy or sanctuary . . .

IV. And be it further enacted, That if any person either within this realm . . . or in any other place out of the Queen's dominions, shall advisedly and with a malicious intent against our said Sovereign Lady, devise and write, print or set forth any manner of book . . . or writing, containing any false seditious and slanderous matter to the defamation of the Queen's Majesty that now is, or to the encouraging . . . of any insurrection or rebellion within this realm . . . ; or if any person . . . either within this realm . . . or in any other place out of the Queen's dominions, shall advisedly and with a malicious intent against our said Sovereign Lady cause any such book . . . or writing to be written, printed, published or set forth, and the said offence not being punishable by the Statute made in the 25th year [1352] of the reign of King Edward the Third concerning treason [&c.] or by any other statute whereby any

offence is made treason, that then every such offence shall be deemed felony, and the offenders therein . . . shall suffer such pains of death and forfeiture as in case of felony is used, without any benefit of clergy or sanctuary . . .

V. And for that divers [several] persons wickedly disposed and forgetting their duty and allegiance have of late not only wished her Majesty's death, but also by divers means practised and sought to know how long her Highness should live, and who should reign after her decease, and what changes and

Mary, Queen of Scots (pictured), was involved in several plots to assassinate Queen Elizabeth.

alterations should thereby happen; . . . be it also enacted, That if any person . . . during the life of our said Sovereign Lady the Queen's Majesty that now is, either within her Highness' dominions or without, shall by setting or erecting any figure or by casting of nativities or by calculation or by any prophesying, witchcraft, conjurations, or other like unlawful means whatsoever, seek to know, and shall set forth by express words, deeds or writings, how long her Majesty shall live, or who shall reign a king or queen of this realm of England after her Highness' decease, or else shall advisedly and with a malicious intent against her Highness, utter any manner of direct prophecies to any such intent, or shall maliciously by any words, writing or printing desire the death or deprivation of our Sovereign Lady the Queen's Majesty that now is . . . that then every such offence shall be felony, and every offender therein, and also all his aiders [&c], shall be judged as felons and shall suffer pains of death and forfeit as in case of felony is used, without any benefit of clergy or sanctuary.

Quoted in G.W. Prothero, ed., *Select Statutes and Other Constitutional Documents Illustrative of the Reigns of Elizabeth and James I.* 4th ed. London: Oxford University Press, 1913. Reprint from *Documents. Reign of Elizabeth. Statute 23 of the Fourth Parliament.*

Parliament Calls for Execution of Mary, Queen of Scots

The rivalry between Elizabeth and her cousin Mary Stuart, Queen of Scots, was long and complex. In 1567 Mary abdicated her Scottish throne and fled to England, where she was a threat to Elizabeth for several reasons: She wanted to succeed Elizabeth, she was fiercely Catholic, and she conspired with local and foreign Catholics to kill Elizabeth. Elizabeth kept Mary imprisoned with tight security. For decades, Elizabeth resisted Parliament's calls for Mary's execution. In the following excerpt, dated November 22, 1586, the members of Parliament express their reasons for calling for Mary's execution.

May it please your most excellent Majesty [Elizabeth], We, your humble, loving and faithful subjects, the Lords and Commons in this present parliament assembled, having of long time, to our intolerable grief, seen by how manifold [many], most dangerous and execrable practices, Mary . . . commonly called the Queen of Scots, hath compassed [plotted] the destruction of your Majesty's sacred and most royal person . . . , and thereby not only to bereave us of the sincere and true religion of Almighty God, bringing us and this noble crown back again into the thraldom [bondage] of the Romish tyranny [tyranny of ancient Rome], but also utterly to ruinate and overthrow the happy state and commonweal [welfare] of this realm: and seeing also what insolent [arrogant] boldness is grown in the heart of the same Queen, through your Majesty's former exceeding favours towards her; and thereupon weighing, with heavy and sorrowful hearts, in what continual peril of suchlike desperate conspiracies and practices your Majesty's most royal and sacred person and life (more dear unto us than our own) is and shall be still, without any possible means to prevent it, so long as the said Scottish Queen shall be suffered to continue [her conspiracy against Elizabeth], and shall not receive that due punishment which, by justice and the laws of this your realm, she hath so often and so many ways, for her most wicked and detestable offences, deserved: therefore . . . We do most humbly beseech your most excellent Majesty that, as well in respect of the continuance of the true religion [Church of England] now professed amongst us and of the safety of your most royal person and estate, as in regard of the preservation and defence of us your most loving, dutiful and faithful subjects and the whole commonweal of this realm, it may please your Highness to take speedy order, that declaration of the same sentence and judgment be made and published by proclamation, and that thereupon direction be given for further proceedings against the said Scottish Queen, according to the effect and true meaning of the said statute [to punish those who threaten the queen's safety]: because, upon advised and great consultation, we cannot find that there is any possible means to provide for your Majesty's safety, but by the just and speedy execution of the said Queen.

Quoted in G.W. Prothero, ed., *Selected Statutes and Other Constitutional Documents Illustrative of the Reigns of Elizabeth and James I.* 4th ed. London: Oxford University Press, 1913. Reprint from Parliamentary Proceedings: General, *D'Ewes' Journals*, pp. 380–402.

Elizabeth Decides the Fate of Mary, Queen of Scots

For many years, Elizabeth resisted Parliament's calls to execute Mary, Queen of Scots. However, following a 1586 conspiracy to assassinate Elizabeth, the third such conspiracy, in which Mary was proven to have been a participant, the English queen decided to give in to Parliament's demand; she felt she had to for her own safety. Mary was executed on February 8, 1587. In the following excerpt, historian William Camden describes how Elizabeth came to her decision.

Yet she [Elizabeth], being a woman naturally slow in her resolutions, began to consider in her mind, whether it were better to put her [Mary, Queen of Scots] to death, or to spare her. As for putting her to death these things were against it: her own innate clemency, lest she should seem to show herself cruel to a woman, and that a princess, and her kinswoman; fear of infamy with posterity in after histories; and imminent and certain dangers as well from the King of Scots, who would now be advanced a step higher in his hopes of England, as from the Catholic princes and desperate men, who would now adventure upon anything. And if she should spare her, she foresaw that no less danger threatened her. The noblemen that had given sentence against the Queen of Scots would endeavor underhand to get into favor with her and her son, not without manifest hazard to herself; the rest of her subjects, who had been so careful for her safety, seeing would not live long, would leave no means untried to hasten Queen Elizabeth's death, that so their religion might be restored.

The courtiers also continually suggested unto her [Elizabeth] these things following, and the like: "Why should you spare her [Mary], when she is guilty and justly condemned, who, though she subscribed to the Association [those committed to protecting Elizabeth] for your safety, yet presently after, resolved unmercifully to ruin you who were altogether innocent, and by destroying you to destroy religion, the nobility and people? Clemency and mercy is a royal virtue, but not to be extended to the merciless. Let the vain show of mercy give place to wholesome severity. Have a care that your unseasonable mercy and favor involve you not in the greatest misery. It is commendation enough of your clemency, to have spared her once: to spare her again were nothing else but to pronounce her guiltless, condemn the estates of the realm of injustice, encourage her favorers to hasten their wicked designs, and discourage your faithful subjects from caring for the commonwealth. Religion, the commonwealth, your own safety, the love of your country, the Oath of Association [vows of those determined to protect Elizabeth] and the care of posterity, do all with their joint prayers beseech you, that she which endangereth the subversion of all these may forthwith be put to death: and except they may prevail, safety itself will never be able to save this commonwealth; and historians will leave it recorded to succeeding ages, that the bright sunshining and glorious days of England under Queen Elizabeth ended in a

Mary is absolved of her sins before being executed for treason in this romanticized painting.

she had frustrated their pains and care, would take it very ill, and for time to come neglect her preservation; many would turn papists [Catholic], and entertain greater hopes, when they should see her preserved as it were by fate to a probability of enjoying the crown; the Jesuits [priests] and seminaries, whose eyes are upon her only, seeing her sickly, and fearing that she foul, cloudy and dark evening, yea in an eternal night . . ." which so troubled and staggered the Queen's mind, that she gave herself wholly over to solitariness, sat many times melancholic and mute, and frequently sighing muttered this to herself, *Aut fer, aut feri*, that is, Either bear with her, or smite her, and, out of I know not what emblem, *Ne feriare, feri*, that is, Strike, lest thou be stricken.

William Camden, *The History of Elizabeth*, 3rd ed. (London, 1675).

Classes of People

During Elizabeth's rule, England had clearly defined social and economic classes. In the following excerpt, political writer Thomas Smith identifies the five classes that existed at the time: major and minor noblemen; esquires, or squires; gentlemen; yeomen, rural freemen rich enough to buy land and accumulate wealth; and, finally, laborers, merchants, and craftsmen, none of whom had a voice in the government.

Of the first part of Gentlemen of England, called *nobilitas major* [major nobility].

. . . In England no man is created a baron [a low-ranking nobleman], except he may dispend [account for] of yearly revenue one thousand pounds, or one thousand marks [in modern values $26,680] at the least . . .

Of the second sort of Gentlemen, which may be called *nobilitas minor* [minor nobility], and first of knights.

No man is a knight by succession, not the king or prince . . . : knights therefore be not born but made . . . In England whosoever may dispend of his free lands forty pounds [$1,600] sterling of yearly revenue . . . may be by the king compelled to take that order and honour, or to pay a fine . . .

Of Esquires.

Esquires (which we commonly call squires) be all those which bear arms (as we call them) or armories . . . these be taken for no

Belonging to the class of major noblemen, the earl of Sussex enjoyed a life of privilege.

distinct order of the commonwealth, but do go with the residue of the gentlemen [classified with gentlemen] . . .

Of Gentlemen.

Gentlemen be those whom their blood and race doth make noble and known . . . Ordinarily the king doth only make knights and create barons or higher degrees, for as for gentlemen they be made good cheap in England. For whosoever studieth the laws of the realm, who studieth in the Universities, who professeth liberal sciences, and to be short, who can live idly and without manual labour, and will bear the port, charge and countenance of a gentleman, he shall be called master, . . . and shall be taken for a gentleman . . .

Of Yeomen.

Those whom we call yeomen, next unto the nobility, knights and squires, have the greatest charge and doings in the commonwealth . . . I call him a yeoman whom our laws do call *legalem hominem* [legal man] . . . which is a freeman born English, and may dispend of his own free land in yearly revenue to the sum of 40s. sterling [$80.00] . . . This sort of people confess themselves to be no gentlemen . . . and yet they have a certain preeminence and more estimation than labourers and artificers [craftsmen], and commonly live wealthily. . . . These be (for the most part) farmers unto gentlemen, . . . and by these means do come to such wealth, that they are able and daily do buy the lands of unthrifty gentlemen, and after setting their sons to the school at the Universities, to the laws of the realm, or otherwise leaving them suffi-

cient lands whereon they may live without labour, do make their said sons by those means gentlemen . . .

Of the fourth sort of men which do not rule [only noblemen may rule].

The fourth sort or class amongst us, is of those which the old Romans called *capite censi* [the lower class] . . . day labourers, poor husbandmen [farmers], yea merchants or retailers which have no free land, copyholders [proofreader's assistant] and all artificers . . . These have no voice nor authority in our commonwealth, and no account is made of them, but only to be ruled.

Thomas Smith, "Classes of People." *Select Statutes and Other Constitutional Documents Illustrative of the Reigns of Elizabeth and James I.* G.W. Prothero, ed. 4th ed. London: Oxford University Press, 1913. Reprint from *The Commonwealth of England,* ed. 1589. Bk. I. Chaps. 17–24.

Laws to Help the Poor

In sixteenth-century England, there was a growing population of poor people requiring support. In an effort to help the poor and to prevent them from begging in the streets, in the early 1560s Parliament enacted laws requiring English citizens to donate money to the cause. The plan began just after Midsummer Day, June 24, 1563. Anyone who refused to help was subject to taxation or imprisonment.

Yearly upon the Sunday next after the feast day of the Nativity of St John Baptist, commonly called Midsummer Day, in every city, borough and town corporate, the mayor, bailiffs or other head officers for the time

Queen Elizabeth presides over a session of Parliament. To help England's poor, Parliament passed laws requiring citizens to give alms.

being, and in every other parish of the country the parson, vicar or curate and churchwardens [officers in the Church of England] shall have written in a register . . . the names of the inhabitants and householders within their city . . . or parish, as also the names of all such impotent, aged and needy persons as be within their city . . . or parish, which are not able to live of themselves nor with their own labour; and shall openly in the church and quietly after divine service call the said householders and inhabitants together,

among whom the mayor or other head officers and two of the chief inhabitants in every such city such as the mayor or other head officers shall think meet, and the parson, vicar or curate and churchwardens in every other parish, shall appoint yearly two able persons or more, to be gatherers and collectors of the charitable alms of all the residue [money that can be collected] of the people inhabiting in the parish whereof they be chosen collectors for the relief of the poor: which collectors the Sunday next after their election, or the Sunday following, if need require, when the people are at the church at divine service, shall gently ask and demand of every man and woman what they of their charity will be contented to give weekly towards the relief of the poor, and the same to be written in the said register . . . : and the said gatherers . . . shall justly gather and truly distribute the same charitable alms weekly . . . to the said poor and impotent persons . . . without fraud, covin [unfairness], favour or affection, and after such sort that the more impotent may have the more help, and such as can get part of their living to have the less, and by the discretion of the collectors to be put in such labour as they be fit and able to do, but none to go or sit openly a-begging upon pain limited in the aforesaid statutes . . .

And be it further enacted, That if any person, being able to further this charitable work, do obstinately refuse reasonably to give towards the help and relief of the poor, or do wilfully discourage other from so charitable a deed, the parson . . . and churchwardens of the parish wherein he dwelleth shall then gently exhort him towards the relief of the poor; and if he will not so be persuaded, then upon the certificate of the parson . . . that the said obstinate person so refusing shall personally appear before the justices of peace of the county . . .

And further be it enacted, That the said justices . . . or the mayor of every such city, if the said obstinate person do appear before them, shall charitably and gently . . . move the said obstinate person to extend his charity towards the relief of the poor of the parish where he dwelleth; and if he . . . will not be persuaded therein . . . that then it shall be lawful for the said justices . . . and . . . for the mayor of the same city with the churchwardens where the said obstinate person shall inhabit, or one of them, to cess [assess], tax and limit upon every such obstinate person so refusing, according to their good discretions, what sum the said obstinate person shall pay weekly towards the relief of the poor . . . ; and if the said person . . . shall refuse to pay the sum that shall be . . . appointed, then the said Justices of Peace . . . or the said mayor shall have full power . . . to commit the said obstinate person . . . to the next gaol [jail] . . .

Quoted in G.W. Prothero, ed., *Selected Statutes and Other Constitutional Documents Illustrative of the Reigns of Elizabeth and James I.* 4th ed. London: Oxford University Press, 1913. Reprint from *Documents. Reign of Elizabeth. Statute 5 of the Second Parliament: First Session.*

Laws Regarding Inheritance

An Elizabethan man who made a will before he died was allowed to distribute his personal property in any way he chose, but distribution of his land was governed by law. According to the law, the eldest son received all of his father's land unless the owner had made prior arrangements. In most cases, the other children got none of the land and were expected to serve their eldest brother after their father's death or try to make a living for themselves. If a man had only daughters, his land was distributed equally among them. In the following document, Elizabethan legal scholar Thomas Smith explains the process.

The testator [one who made a legally valid will before death] disposeth in his last will his moveable goods freely as he thinketh meet [appropriate] and convenient without controlment of wife or children. And our testaments [English traditions] for goods moveable be not subject to the ceremonies of the civil law, but made with all liberty and freedom. . . . Of lands as ye have understood before, there is difference: for when the owner dieth, his land descendeth only to his eldest son, all the rest both sons and daughters have nothing by the common law, but must serve their eldest brother if they will, or make what other shift they can to live: except that [unless] the father in life time do make some conveyance and estates of part of his land to their use, or else by devise, which word amongst our lawyers doth betoken a testament written, sealed, and delivered in the life time of the testator before witness: for without those ceremonies a bequest of lands is not available. But by the common law if he that dieth hath no sons but daughters, the land is equally divided among them, which portion is made by agreement or by lot. Although as I have said ordinarily and by the common law, the eldest son inheriteth all the lands, yet in some countries all the sons have equal portion, and that is called ganelkinde, and is in many places in Kent [in southeast England]. In some places the youngest is sole heir: and in some places after an other fashion. But these being but particular customs of certain places and out of the rule of the common law, do little appertain [pertain] to the disputation of the policy of the whole realm, and may be infinite. The common wealth is judged by that which is most ordinarily and commonly done through the whole realm.

Thomas Smith, *De Republica Anglorum: The Manner of Government or Policy of the Realm of England, 1583.*

Chapter

3

Entertainment and Literature

One of the most notable contributions to come out of Elizabethan England was a respect and love of the arts. Before Elizabeth's reign, England had endured centuries of decline, disease, and poverty. People worked hard and had little time or money to spare for entertainment. As the country prospered under Elizabeth's guiding hand, however, more and more people—from the queen herself to the commoners she ruled—had increasingly more time and money to spend on leisure activities.

Certainly, the most famous type of entertainment to come out of Elizabethan England was the theater. Although plays had been performed for years before Elizabeth took the throne, they generally featured religious themes. During the mid-to-late sixteenth century, however, plays took on more secular and dramatic themes. These included love, betrayal, and political conspiracy. The stories were exciting, and people flocked to performances. Groups of actors traveled around the city and countryside performing in courtyards, inns, or wherever people could gather.

As the sixteenth century progressed, the traveling actors formed acting companies and built permanent theaters so they could put on their plays for more and larger audiences. In 1576, actor James Burbage built the first permanent theater, called simply the Theatre, in Shoreditch, a London suburb. Other theaters followed, and by the turn of the seventeenth century, there were eight permanent theaters in England.

These permanent theaters, because they were generally owned by playwrights and actors, tended to concentrate on presenting the works of certain authors. For example, the Globe, perhaps the country's most famous theater, put on many of the plays of one of the era's most famous playwrights. William Shakespeare, a young writer and actor, appeared on the theater scene in the late sixteenth century. Shakespeare was born in 1564 in Stratford-upon-Avon, a town outside Birmingham.

He arrived in London a little over twenty years later and joined a company of actors called the King's Men. While performing with that company, he wrote many of the plays that would make him famous. His best known works include *Romeo and Juliet, Hamlet, Othello,* and *A Midsummer Night's Dream.*

William Shakespeare was not the only well-known Elizabethan playwright, however. There were many others whose works became famous during the era. Christopher Marlowe, John Donne, Robert Greene, and John Lyly are some of the most

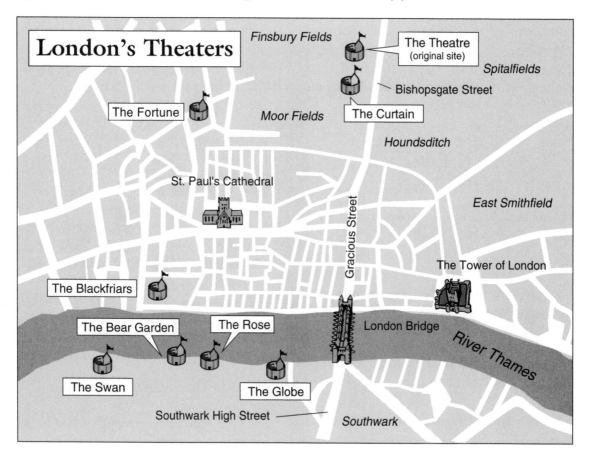

London's Theaters

famous. Some of these men were university educated; others, like Shakespeare, were self-taught. In any case, all wrote plays that appealed to and entertained a wide audience. Everyone from courtiers to merchants flocked weekly to London's theaters to see the creations of these men, and Elizabeth herself often had them perform their plays at her palace.

Many of these men were not only playwrights, they were poets as well. Poetry flourished during the reign of Elizabeth, and many new forms of poetry took shape. One of the most popular of these new forms was the sonnet. Sonnets are fourteen-line poems that usually express the writer's love and admiration for a beautiful woman. Often, Elizabethan writers wrote whole series of sonnets or other poems about the same woman; in some cases, the poems were written about the queen herself.

The flowering in the arts that took place during the Elizabethan era cannot obscure the fact that many Elizabethans enjoyed cruder forms of entertainment. In particular, they liked violent, exciting sports. One of the most popular was called bearbaiting. Bearbaiting pitted a restrained bear against attacking dogs. Crowds cheered the dogs on, and the spectacle ended only when the bear was moments from death.

During her reign, Elizabeth supported the English people in their love of fun and entertainment. The documents in this chapter reflect the types of entertainment Elizabeth and her subjects enjoyed.

Queen Elizabeth, the Poet

Elizabeth was not only a sixteenth-century queen; she was also a poet. In the following poem, "When I Was Fair and Young," Elizabeth writes that she was thoughtless with suitors when she was beautiful and young, but that as she got older, she regretted that behavior.

When I Was Fair and Young

When I was fair and young, and favor
  gracèd me,
Of many was I sought, their mistress for
  to be;

But I did scorn them all, and answered
  them therefore,
  Go, go, go, seek some otherwhere,
    Impòrtune me no more!
How many weeping eyes I made to pine
  with woe,
How many sighing hearts, I have no skill
  to show;
Yet I the prouder grew, and answered
  them therefore,
  Go, go, go, seek some otherwhere,
    impòrtune me no more!

Then spake fair Venus' son, that proud
  victorious boy,
  And said: Fine dame, since that you be so
  coy,

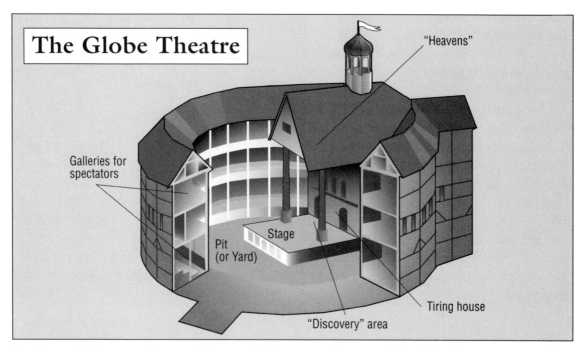

The Globe Theatre

"Heavens"

Galleries for spectators

Stage

Pit (or Yard)

Tiring house

"Discovery" area

I will so pluck your plumes that you shall say no more,
  Go, go, go, seek some otherwhere,
    Impòrtune me no more!

When he had spake these words, such change grew in my breast
That neither night nor day since that, I could take any rest.
Then lo! I did repent that I had said before,
  Go, go, go, seek some otherwhere,
    Impòrtune me no more!

Queen Elizabeth, "When I Was Fair and Young." *The Rawlinson Poetry Ms. 85.* Bodleian Library, Oxford, U.K.

Payments to Actors

Shakespeare's company of actors, the King's Men, received money from Elizabeth's royal court. The following excerpts reflect two payments the company received in 1603. In the first, the court treasurer paid the company during the plague epidemic, when the theaters were closed to prevent the spread of illness. The second record shows that the treasurer paid the company for performances at two religious holiday celebrations.

To Richard Burbadg [a member of the company] one of his ma^te [majesty's] Comedians vppon the Councelle warraunte dated at Hamptoncourte viij^o die [eighth day of] Februarij 1603 for the mayntenaunce and releife of himselfe and the rest of his Company being prohibited to p^rsente any playes publiquelie in or neere London by reason of great perill that might growe throughe the extraordinary

Concourse and assemblie of people to a newe increase of the plague till it shall please god to settle the Cittie in a more pfecte health by way of his Maties free gifte xxx^li [30£].

To Iohn Hemynge [a member of the company] one of his ma^te players vppon the Councelle warraunte dated at the Courte at Whitehall vltimo die [last day of] Februar' 1603 for himselfe and the rest of his Company for two playes p^rsented before his ma^tie viz [namely] the one on Candelmas Day at night and the other on Shrouesonday at night the some of thirtene poundes six shilling and eight pence and way of his ma^te rewarde for the same twoe playes six poundes thirteene shilling and iiij^or pence in all the some of xx^li.

Quoted in Russ McDonald, *The Bedford Companion to Shakespeare: An Introduction with Documents.* Boston: Bedford Books of St. Martin's Press, 1996.

Inventory of Theatrical Costumes

This list of theatrical costumes, probably compiled in 1602, was written by Edward Alleyn, a tragedian who acted with a troupe called Lord Admiral's Men. The inventory includes cloaks, gowns, and other attire. It is transcribed in the original spelling and

An eighteenth-century painting depicts a scene from Shakespeare's Taming of the Shrew. *Elizabethan actors used ornate costuming to lend color and authenticity to plays.*

marked with parentheses in places where the original inventory was incomplete.

1 A scarlett cloke wth ij [2] brode gould Laces: w^t [with] gould buttens of the sam downe the sids
2 A black velvett cloke
   A scarlett cloke Layd (the)[1] downe w^t silver Lace and silver buttens
4 A short velvett cap clok embroydered w^t gould and gould spangles
5 A watshod [watchet, light blue] sattins clok w^t v gould laces
6 A pur(l)pell sattin w^elted [welted, bordered] w^t velvett and silver twist
7 A bla*ck*[2] tufted cloke cloke
8 A dama*s*k cloke garded cloke garded [guarded, trimmed] w^t velvett
   A longe blak tafata cloke
   A colored bugell [beaded cloak?] for aboye
   A scarlett w^t buttens of gould fact [faced, trimmed] w^t blew velvett
12 A scarlett fact w^t blak velvett
13 A stamell [red] cloke w^t (b)gould lace
14 blak bugell cloke

Gownes

(1 hary ye viij gowne
2 the blak velvett gowne w^t wight fure
3 A crimosin Robe strypt w^t gould fact w^t ermin
4 on of wrought cloth of gould
5 on of red silk w^t gould butt*ens*
(6 a cardinalls gowne

7 wemens gowns
8 i blak velvett embroyde
9 w^t gould
10 i cloth of gould candish [Cavendish?, an actor or role] his *s*tuf
11 blak velvett lact and drawne owt w^t wight sarsnett [silk fabric]
12 A black silk w^t red flush
13 A cloth of silver for pan [Parr?, an actor]
14 a yelow silk gowne
(15 a red silk gowne
(16 angels silk
17 ij blew calico gowns

Antik sutes [clown suits, motley]

1 a cote of crimosen velvett cutt in payns and embryderd in gould
2 i cloth of gould cote w^t grene bases [skirts]
3 i cloth of goul*d* cote w^t oraingtawny bases
4 i cloth of go<..>[3] silver cott w^t blewe silk & tinsell bases
5 i blew damask cote the more
6 a red velvett hors mans cote
7 A yelow tafata pd [?]
8 cloth of gould horsmans cote
9 cloth *of* bodkin [baudekin, rich fabric] hormans cote
10 orayngtany horsmans cot of cloth lact
11 daniels gowne
12 blew embroyderde bases
13 will somers [Will Summers, an actor] cote
14 wight embroyd bases

[1.] Parentheses indicate deletions or alterations.
[2.] Italic letters indicate difficult readings, cut off or blotted letters in the original.

[3.] Pointed brackets indicate letters or words that are illegible, mutilated, or cut away in the original.

15 (g) gilt lether cot
16 ij hedtirs [head tires, tiaras] sett w^t stons
17

Jerkings and dublets

1 A crymosin velvett pd w^t gould buttens & lace
2 a crymasin sattin case [fitted jacket] lact w^t gould lace all over
(3 A velvett dublett cut di*a*mond lact w^t gould lace and spang [small ornament]
4 a dublett of blak velvett cut [slashed ornamentally] on sillver tinsell
5 A ginger colored dublett
6 i wight sattin cute onwight
7 blak velvett w^t gould lace
8 green velvett
9 blak tafata cut on blak velvett lacte w^t bugell
10 blak velvett playne
11 ould wight sattin
12 red velvett for a boye
13 A carnation velvett lacte w^t silver
14 A yelow spangled case
15 red velvett w^t blew sattin sleves & case
16 cloth of silver Jerkin
17 faustus [Faustus, Marlowe's tragic character] Jerkin his clok

1 frenchose
blew velvett embr w^t gould paynes
blew sattin scalin [unidentified garment]
2 silver paynes lact w^t carnation satins lact over w^t silver
3 the guises [masks]
(4 Rich payns [strips of cloth] w^t Long *stok*ins
5 gould payns w^t blak stript scalings of ca*nis* [?]

6 gould payns w^t velvett scalings
7 gould payns w^t red strypt scalings
8 black bugell
9 red payns for a boy w^t yelo scalins
10 pryams hoes [Priam's hose]
11 spangled hoes

venetians

(1 A purple velvett cut in dimonds Lact & spangels
2 red velved lact w^t gould spanish
(3 a purpell velvet emproydored w^t silver cut on tinse*l*
4 green velvett lact w^t gould spanish
5 blake velvett
6 cloth of silver
7 gren strypt sattin
8 cloth of gould for a boye

Henslowe's Papers, 1602.

Juliet Expresses Her Longing for Romeo

William Shakespeare was one of the period's most famous playwrights and poets. The following excerpt is from his play, Romeo and Juliet. *Here Juliet speaks from her balcony, and Romeo hears her from the orchard below. Juliet declares that their family names should be set aside for their love.*

JUL. O Romeo, Romeo! wherefore art thou Romeo?
Deny thy father and refuse thy name!
Or, if thou wilt not, be but sworn my love,
And I'll no longer be a Capulet.

ROM. [*aside*] Shall I hear more, or shall I speak at this?

JUL. 'Tis but thy name that is my enemy.
Thou art thyself, though not a Montague.
What's Montague? It is nor hand, nor foot,
Nor arm, nor face, nor any other part
Belonging to a man. O, be some other name!
What's in a name? That which we call a rose
By any other name would smell as sweet.
So Romeo would, were he not Romeo call'd,
Retain that dear perfection which he owes
Without that title. Romeo, doff thy name;
And for that name, which is no part of thee,
Take all myself.

ROM. I take thee at thy word.
Call me but love, and I'll be new baptiz'd [named];
Henceforth I never will be Romeo.

JUL. What man art thou that, thus bescreen'd [hidden] in night,
So stumblest on my counsel [advice]?

ROM. By a name
I know not how to tell thee who I am.
My name, dear saint, is hateful to myself,
Because it is an enemy to thee.
Had I it written, I would tear the word.

JUL. My ears have yet not drunk [heard] a hundred words
Of that tongue's utterance, yet I know the sound.
Art thou not Romeo, and a Montague?

ROM. Neither, fair saint, if either thee dislike.

JUL. How cam'st thou hither, tell me, and wherefore?
The orchard walls are high and hard to climb,
And the place death [dangerous], considering who thou art,
If any of my kinsmen find thee here.

ROM. With love's light wings did I o'erperch [jump over] these walls.

William Shakespeare, *The Tragedy of Romeo and Juliet,* 1594.

The Royal License for Shakespeare's Company

In 1603 King James I (who succeeded Elizabeth when she died) offered this license to William Shakespeare's theater company, Lord Chamberlain's Men, also called the King's Men.

We . . . do license and authorize these our Servants Lawrence Fletcher, William Shakespeare, Richard Burbage, Augustine Phillips, John Heminges, Henry Condell, William Sly, Robert Armin, Richard Cowley, and the rest of their associates freely to use and exercise the art and faculty of playing comedies, tragedies, histories, interludes, morals, pastorals, stageplays, and such others like as they have already studied or hereafter shall use or study as well for the recreation of our loving subjects as for our solace and pleasure when we shall think good to see them during our pleasure.

Royal License for Shakespeare's Company, 1603.

Puritan Criticism of the Theater

People occasionally criticized the theaters, but the Puritans, a religious group that held strict beliefs about morality, launched the loudest, most severe attacks. In the following excerpt, Philip Stubbes, a vocal Puritan spokesman, attacks the public theaters as immoral and urges the actors to seek more godly lines of work.

Do they [actors] not maintain bawdry, insinuate foolery, and renew and remembrance of heathen idolatry [paganism]? Do they not induce whoredom and uncleanness and nay, are they not rather plain devourers of maidenly virginity and chastity? For proof whereof, but mark the flocking and running to theaters and curtains, daily and hourly, night and day, time and tide, to see plays and interludes, where such wanton gestures, such bawdy speeches, such laughing and fleering [ridiculing], such kissing and bussing, such clipping and culling [gathering], such winking and glancing of wanton eyes and the like is used, as is wonderful to behold. Then the godly pageants being done, every mate sorts to his mate, every one brings another homeward of their way very friendly, and in their secret conclaves (covertly) they play the Sodomites [biblical people who were destroyed because of their wickedness], or worse. And these be the fruits of plays and interludes, for the most part. And whereas, you say, there are good examples to be learned in them.

Truly, so there are. If you [the reader] will learn falsehood, if you will learn cozenage [deceit]; if you will learn to play the hypocrite; to cog [cheat], lie, and falsify; if you will learn to jest, laugh, and fleer [smirk], to grin, to nod, and mow [jest]; if you will learn to play the vice, to swear, tear, and blaspheme both heaven and earth. If you will learn to become a bawd, unclean, and to devirginate maids, to de-

William Prynne was an influential Puritan pamphleteer who crusaded against the public theater.

flower honest wives; if you will learn to murder, slay, kill, pick, steal, rob, and rove [wander]; if you will learn to rebel against princes, to commit treasons, to consume treasures, to practice idleness, to sing and talk of bawdy love and venery [sex]; if you will learn to deride, scoff, mock, and flout, to flatter and smooth; if you will learn to play the whoremaster, the glutton, drunkard, or incestuous person; if you will learn to become proud, haughty, and arrogant; and finally, if you will learn to contemn [despise] God and all his laws, to care neither for heaven nor hell, and to commit all kind of sin and mischief, you need to go to no other school, for all these good examples may you see painted before your eyes in interludes and plays. . . .

Therefore I beseech all players and founders of plays and interludes, in the bowels [seat of pity] of Jesus Christ, as they tender the salvation of their souls, and others, to leave off that cursed kind of life and give themselves to such honest exercises and godly mysteries as God hath commanded them in his word to get their livings withal. For who will call him a wise man that playeth the part of a fool and a vice? Who can call him a Christian who playeth the part of a devil, the sworn enemy of Christ? Who can call him a just man that playeth the part of a dissembling hypocrite? And to be brief, who can call him a straight-dealing man, who playeth a cozener's trick? And so of all the rest. Away therefore with this so infamous an art, for go they never so brave [no matter how splendid they appear], yet are they count-

ed and taken but for beggars. And is it not true? Live they not upon beggings of every one that comes? Are they not taken by the laws of the realm for rogues and vagabonds? I speak of such as travel the countries with plays and interludes, making an occupation of it, and ought to be punished, if they had their deserts.

Philip Stubbes, *The Anatomy of Abuses,* 1583.

Shakespeare Dedicates Poems to Southampton

During Elizabeth's time, writers gained favor and financial support from the court by writing poems in praise of the queen or one of her favorite courtiers. In these poems, writers also spoke humbly about themselves. In the following excerpts, William Shakespeare dedicates poems to the earl of Southampton, one of Queen Elizabeth's courtiers. In the first, published on April 18, 1593, Shakespeare criticizes his own work and offers extravagant praise in honor of the earl. In the second, published on May 9, 1594, he affirms his love for the earl and assures him of his continued duty.

April 18, 1593
To the Right Honourable Henrie Wriothesley, Earle of Southampton, and Baron of Titchfield.

Right Honourable, I know not how I shall offend in dedicating my vnpolisht lines to your Lordship, nor how the worlde will censure mee for choosing so strong a

William Shakespeare (pictured) owed his success in part to the support of courtiers like the earl of Southampton.

proppe to support so weake a burthen, one-lye if your Honour seeme but pleased, I account my selfe highly praised, and vowe to take aduantage of all idle houres, till I haue honoured you with some grauer labour. But if the first heire of my inuention proue deformed, I shall be sorie it had so noble a god-father: and neuer after eare so barren a land, for feare it yeeld me still so bad a haruest. I leave it to your Honourable suruey, and your Honor to your hearts content, which I wish may alwaies answere your owne wish, and the worlds hopefull expectation.

Your Honors in all dutie,
William Shakespeare

May 9, 1594

To the Right Honourable, Henry Wriothesley, Earle of Southampton, and Baron of Titchfield.

The loue I dedicate to your Lordship is without end: wherof this Pamphlet without beginning is but a superfluous Moity [part]. The warrant I haue of your Honourable disposition, not the worth of my vntutord Lines makes it assured of acceptance. What I haue done is yours, what I haue to doe is yours, being part in all I haue, devoted yours. Were my worth greater, my duety would shew greater, meane time, as it is, it is bound to your Lordship; To whom I wish long life still lengthened with all happinesse.

Your Lordships in all duety.
William Shakespeare

William Shakespeare, "Venus and Adonis" (1593) and "The Rape of Lucrece" (1594).

The First Reference to Shakespeare in Print

In a pamphlet written shortly before his death, Robert Greene bemoans the lack of attention given to him as a playwright and criticizes the new playwrights, particularly William Shakespeare. In this excerpt, the first known reference to Shakespeare in print, Greene calls the young man "an upstart Crow," implying that Shakespeare is an uneducated novice. He also says that Shakespeare is "beautified with our feathers," suggesting that he depends on other playwrights for his lines. The jack-of-all-trades line suggests that Shakespeare is shallow. And Greene closes by identifying his friends (and by implication himself) as "rare wits" and the newcomers as "Apes" and "rude groomes."

If wofull experience may moue you (Gentlemen) to beware, or vnheard of wretchednes intreate you to take heed: I doubt not but you wil looke backe with sorrow on your time past, and indeuour with repentance to spend that which is to come. Wonder not, (for with thee wil I first begin) thou famous gracer of Tragedians, that *Greene,* who hath said with thee (like the foole in his heart) There is no God, shoulde now giue/glorie vnto his greatnes: for penetrating is his power, his hand lyes heauie vpon me, hee hath spoken vnto mee with a voice of thunder, and I haue felt he is a God that can punish enemies. Why should thy excellent wit, his gift, bee so blinded, that thou shouldst giue no glorie to the giuer? . . .

With thee I ioyne yong *Iuuenall,* that byting [Roman] Satyrist, that lastly with mee together writ a Comedie. / Sweet boy, might I aduise thee, be aduisde, and get not many enemies by bitter wordes: inueigh against vaine men, for thou canst do it, no man better, no man so well: thou hast a libertie to reprooue all, and name none; for one being spoken to, all are offended; none being blamed no man is iniured. Stop shallow water still running, it will rage, or tread on a worme and it will turne: then blame not Schollers vexed with sharpe lines, if they reproue thy too much liberty of reproofe. . . .

Base minded men all three of you, if by my miserie you be not warnd: for vnto none of you (like mee) sought those burres to cleaue: those Puppets (I meane) that spake from our mouths, those Anticks garnisht in our colours. Is it not strange, that I, to whom they all haue beene beholding: is it not like that you, to whome they all haue beene beholding, shall (were yee in that case as I am now) bee both at once of them forsaken? Yes trust them not: for there is an vpstart Crow, beautified with our feathers, that with his *Tygers hart wrapt in a Players hyde,* supposes he is as well able to bombast out a blanke verse as the best of you: and beeing an absolute *Iohannes fac totum* [jack-of-all-trades], is in his owne conceit the onely Shake-scene in a countrey. O that I might intreat your rare wits to be imploied in more profitable courses: & let those Apes imitate your past excellence, and neuer more acquaint them with your admired inuentions. I knowe the best husband of/you all will neuer proue an Vsurer, and the kindest of them all will neuer proue a kind nurse: yet whilest you may, seeke you better Maisters; for it is pittie men of such rare wits, should be subject to the pleasure of such rude groomes.

Robert Greene, *Groats-worth of Witte: The Repentance of Robert Greene.* London: William Wright, 1592.

Jonson Pays Tribute to Shakespeare

Elizabethan playwright Ben Jonson harshly criticized William Shakespeare's writing style while Shakespeare was alive. However, seven years after Shakespeare's death, Jonson wrote a poem for the First Folio edition of Shakespeare's plays published in 1623. Entitled "To the Memory of My Beloved Master, William Shakespeare," the poem praises Shakespeare as a genius, greater than other English writers and greater even than the ancient Greek and Roman playwrights.

Soul of the age!
The applause, delight, the wonder of our
　stage!
My Shakespeare, rise! I will not lodge thee
　by
Chaucer, or Spenser, or bid Beaumont lie
A little farther off, to make thee a room: [1]
Thou art a monument without a tomb,
And art alive still while thy book doth live
And we have wits to read and praise to
　give.
That I not mix thee so, my brain excuses,
I mean with great, but disproportioned
　Muses;
For if I thought my judgment were of
　years,
I should commit thee surely with thy
　peers,
And tell how far thou didst our Lyly out-
　shine,
Or sporting Kyd, or Marlowe's [2] mighty
　line.
And though thou hadst small Latin and
　less Greek,

From thence to honor thee, I would not
　seek
For names; but call forth thundering
　Æschylus,
Euripides, and Sophocles [3] to us;
Pacuvius, Accius, him of Cordova dead, [4]
To life again, to hear thy buskin [5] tread,
And shake a stage; or, when thy socks
　were on,
Leave thee alone for the comparison
Of all that insolent Greece or haughty
　Rome
Sent forth, or since did from their ashes
　come.
Triumph, my Britain, thou hast one to
　show
To whom all scenes of Europe homage
　owe.
He [Shakespeare] was not of an age, but
　for all time!
And all the Muses still were in their prime,
When, like Apollo, he came forth to warm
Our ears, or like a Mercury to charm!
Nature herself was proud of his designs
And joyed to wear the dressing of his
　lines!
Which were so richly spun, and woven so
　fit,
As, since, she will vouchsafe [grant] no
　other wit. . . .
Sweet Swan of Avon! [Shakespeare lived in
　the English town of Avon] what a sight it
　were
To see thee in our waters yet appear,

[1] These poets need not make room for Shakespeare near their graves; he does not need to be buried with them to ensure his fame.
[2] three Elizabethan playwrights
[3] the three great Greek writers of tragedy
[4] Roman tragedians
[5] a thick-soled boot

The Popular Elizabethan Sonnet

The sonnet, a fourteen-line poem expressing love or admiration for someone special, became a popular type of poem in Elizabethan England. There are two ways a sonnet can be written. In one form, the first eight lines present a doubt, a problem, a question, or a desire that is resolved in the last six lines. In the second form, the sonnet's subject matter appears in the first twelve lines, and the last two lines present a resolution. In the following sonnet, poet Philip Sidney employs the second technique. He tells in the first twelve lines how he won first place in a riding tournament and how the audience discusses his skill. In the last two lines, he attributes his success to his love for a beautiful woman named Stella.

Ben Jonson (pictured), a contemporary of Shakespeare, is the author of a poem praising the dramatist's genius.

And make those flights upon the banks of
  Thames,
That so did take Eliza [Queen Elizabeth],
  and our James! [Elizabeth's successor,
  James I]
But stay, I see thee in the hemisphere
Advanced, and made a constellation
  there!
Shine forth, thou Star of poets, and with
  rage
Or influence, chide or cheer the drooping
  stage,
Which, since thy flight from hence, hath
  mourned like night,
And despairs day, but for thy volume's
  light.

Ben Jonson, "To the Memory of My Beloved Master."
First Folio, 1623.

Having this day my horse, my hand, my
  lance
Guided so well that I obtained the prize
Both by the judgment of the English eyes
And of some sent from that sweet enemy
  France,
Horsemen my skill in horsemanship
  advance,
Town folks my strength; a daintier judge
  applies
His praise to sleight [trick] which from
  good use doth rise;
Some lucky wits impute it but to chance;
Others, because of both sides I do take
My blood from them who did excel in
  this,
Think Nature me a man-at-arms did make.
How far they shot awry! the true cause is,

Stella looked on, and from her heavenly
    face
Sent forth the beams which made so fair
    my race.

Philip Sidney, "Sonnet 41" from *Astrophel and Stella*
(1591).

Marlowe's Love Poem

Christopher Marlowe was another famous poet and playwright in Elizabethan England. The following is one of his most famous love poems, "The Passionate Shepherd to His Love." In the poem, the speaker promises the woman he loves a pleasurable life and fine clothes if she will be his.

This is the only known portrait of Christopher Marlowe, a popular Elizabethan poet and playwright.

Come live with me and be my Love,
And we will all the pleasures prove
That hills and valleys, dales and fields,
Or woods or steepy mountain yields.
And we will sit upon the rocks,
And see the shepherds feed their flocks
By shallow rivers, to whose falls
Melodious birds sing madrigals.

And I will make thee beds of roses
And a thousand fragrant posies;
A cap of flowers, and a kirtle [skirt]
Embroidered all with leaves of myrtle;

A gown made of the finest wool
Which from our pretty lambs we pull;
Fair-linèd slippers for the cold,
With buckles of the purest gold;

A belt of straw and ivy buds
With coral clasps and amber studs—
And if these pleasures may thee move,
Come live with me and be my Love.

The shepherd swains [young men] shall
    dance and sing
For thy delight each May morning—
If these delights thy mind may move,
Then live with me and be my Love.

Christopher Marlowe, "The Passionate Shepherd to His
Love," 1599.

Dekker's Prologue to the Queen

Elizabethan writers often praised the queen and belittled themselves in their work. Here, Thomas Dekker, an Elizabethan journalist, poet, and playwright, employs that style. The following excerpt is the prologue to his play

A satirical woodcut depicts Robert Greene at his writing desk dressed as a pear. Greene was ridiculed by contemporaries for his illegible handwriting.

The Shoemaker's Holiday, *in which an actor addresses the queen before the play begins. He praises her, begs for her smile, and says that without it, the actors cannot live.*

As wretches in a storm, expecting day,
With trembling hands and eyes cast up to
  heaven,
Make prayers the anchor of their con-
  quered hopes,
So we, dear goddess, wonder of all eyes,
Your meanest vassels, through mistrust and
  fear
To sink into the bottom of disgrace
By our imperfect pastimes, prostrate thus
On bended knees, our sails of hope do
  strike [lower],
Dreading the bitter storms of your dislike.
Since then, unhappy men, our hap [for-
  tune] is such

That to ourselves ourselves no help can
  bring,
But needs must perish, if your saint-like
  ears,
Locking the temple where all mercy sits,
Refuse the tribute of our begging
  tongues;
Oh grant, bright mirror of true chastity,
From those life-breathing stars, your sun-
  like eyes,
One gracious smile; for your celestial
  breath
Must send us life, or sentence us to death.

Thomas Dekker, "The Shoemaker's Holiday" (1599).

The Publisher Amends Greene's Manuscript

In Elizabethan England, the publishing business was a young industry struggling to develop techniques that insured accuracy. In this excerpt, publisher Henry Chettle describes his efforts to remain true to the writings of author Robert Greene while preparing an essay of Greene's for publication. Because Greene's handwriting was often illegible and Greene had died, Chettle had to recopy the manuscript for the typographer. He says he followed the original as closely as he could and claims to have deleted only material that he thought Greene would have wanted eliminated, but not to have added anything.

At the perusing of Greene's booke, [I] stroke out [deleted] what then in conscience I thought that he in some displeasure writ, or, had it beene true, yet to publish it was intollerable, him I would wish to use me no worse than I deserve. I had onely in the copy this share: it was il written, as sometimes Greenes hand was none of the best; licensd it must be, ere it could bee printed, which could never be if it might not be reade: to be briefe, I writ it over, and, as neare as I could, followed the copy, only in that letter I put something out, but in the whole booke not a worde in, for I protest it was all Greenes, not mine. . . . as some unjustly have affirmed.

Henry Chettle, *Kind Hart's Dream,* 1592.

A Printer Warns Authors About Inaccurate Manuscripts

Standards of accuracy in publishing were high when the printing press first came to England during the late 1400s, but they had declined by Elizabeth's time. Sixteenth-century printers no longer hired correctors (proofreaders), as earlier printers had, and compositors (typesetters) did not take responsibility for accuracy. In the following excerpt, printer Joseph Moxon urges authors to prepare accurate, legible, and well-marked manuscripts and not to expect the typesetter to make alterations unless the authors are willing to pay the typesetter additional fees.

"Although I have in the precedent Exercises shew'd the Accomplishments of a good Compositer [typesetter], yet will not a curious Author trust either to his Care or Abilities in Printing, Italicking, Capitalling, Breaking, &c. Therefore it behoves an Author to examine his Copy very well e're he deliver it to the Printer and to Point it, and mark it so as the Compositer may know what Words to Set in Italick, English, Capitals, &c." The copy should be perfect; "for by no means he ought to hope to mend it in the Proof, the Compositer not being obliged to it; And it cannot reasonably be expected he should be so good Natured to take so much pains to mend such Alterations as the second Dictates of an Author may make, unless he be very well paid for it over and above what he agreed for with the Master-Printer."

Quoted in Evelyn May Albright, *Dramatic Publications in England, 1580–1640: A Study of Conditions Affecting Content and Form of Drama.* New York: Gordian, 1971.

Bearbaiting

One of the many forms of entertainment the people in Elizabethan England enjoyed was bearbaiting. Bearbaiting took place in an arena. Dogs fought bears that were often tied to a stake until the bears were in danger of being killed; at that point the animals were separated. In the following excerpt, writer Lupold von Wedel describes his visit to a bearbaiting arena.

The Thames is crossed by a bridge [London Bridge] leading to another town on the other side of the water called Sedorck [Southwark]. This bridge is built

Bearbaiting was a popular form of entertainment in Elizabethan England. Here, a bear beset by dogs has broken its chain and threatens a crowd of spectators.

of stone, 470 paces long, but its upper part has not the appearance of a bridge, being entirely set with fine houses filled with all kinds of wares, very nice to look at. . . .

On the 23rd we went across the bridge to the above-mentioned town. There is a round building three stories high, in which are kept about a hundred large English dogs, with separate wooden kennels for each of them. These dogs were made to fight singly with three bears, the second bear being larger than the first, and the third larger than the second. After this a horse was brought in and chased by the dogs, and at last a bull, who defended himself bravely. The next was that a number of men and women came forward from a separate compartment, dancing, conversing, and fighting with each other; also a man who threw some white bread among the crowd, that scrambled for it. Right over the middle of the place a rose was fixed, this rose being set on fire by a rocket: suddenly lots of apples and pears fell out of it down upon the people standing below. Whilst the people were scrambling for the apples, some rockets were made to fall down upon them out of the rose, which caused a great fright but amused the spectators. After this, rockets and other fireworks came flying out of all corners, and that was the end of the play.

Lupold von Wedel, "A Visit to the Bearbaiting Arena." From *Journey through England and Scotland,* trans. Gottfried von Bulow, 1584–85.

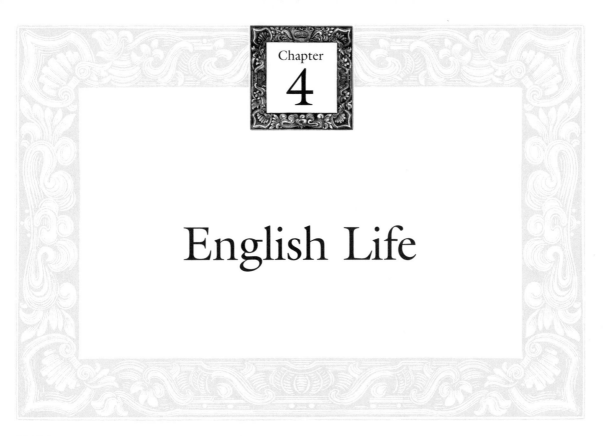

English Life

For many people, life in Elizabethan England was hard and dangerous. Plagues swept though London, killing entire families. Criminals of all types lurked about, ready to rob or assault passersby. Even the candles and fireplaces residents used to light and heat their homes posed a threat; having one's home consumed by fire was a constant danger.

These perils affected everyone. A person's wealth or social standing made no difference. Disease, for example, cared little if its victims were wealthy or poor. As the sixteenth century unfolded, plagues killed thousands of Elizabeth's subjects. Crime also did not discriminate. London's streets were dangerous places, populated by thieves and disreputable characters.

Anyone traversing the city streets at night was likely to be attacked or robbed. And infant mortality rates were high; most children, wealthy or poor, died before they reached the age of ten.

Even though all citizens were vulnerable to these things, in general, the wealthier a person was, the less likely he or she was to suffer. Wealthy people enjoyed lives of luxury and privilege. Many owned airy country estates and employed servants to run their households. They sent their children to good schools and indulged in fashionable clothes. Poorer people, on the other hand, lived in cramped city housing and spent most of their time working. Farmers toiled long hours in their fields. Merchants peddled wares on city streets.

A family member comforts a well-to-do victim of plague, as servants work to make his final hours as comfortable as possible.

And poor children had little if any schooling; they had to work alongside their parents to help support their families.

The vast division between rich and poor was a result of England's being a class society. This meant the population was divided into several social groups, or classes. The wealthiest groups were members of the higher classes. They were considered most important, and it was their influence that Elizabeth considered when deciding governmental policy. The poorer groups were members of the lower classes. These people had no say in government and little opportunity to improve their social situation.

Not all aspects of Elizabethan life were so ominous, however. There were some enjoyable events, but class generally affected these as well. Many families gathered to attend weddings, mark the births of children, and celebrate holidays, but the manner in which they did so was dictated by social class. Wealthy people, for example, generally hosted extravagant wedding receptions, while the poor made do with more modest affairs. The documents in this chapter illustrate the celebrations Elizabethans enjoyed, the differences and similarities of life for the social classes, and many of the hardships the Elizabethans faced as they went through their daily lives.

Freedom for Married Women

Elizabethan men had tremendous power over their wives. Even so, English men gave their wives more independence than men in other countries. In this document, Dutch writer

Van Meteren describes English women's freedom to shop, to employ servants for housework, and to spend their days socializing with neighbors and friends.

Wives in England are entirely in the power of their husbands, their lives only excepted

. . . yet they are not kept so strictly as they are in Spain or elsewhere. Nor are they shut up, but they have the free management of the house or housekeeping, after the fashion of those of the Netherlands, and others their neighbours. They go to market to buy what they like best to eat. They are well dressed, fond of taking it easy, and commonly leave the care of household matters and drudgery to their servants. They sit before their doors, decked out in fine clothes, in order to see and be seen by the passers-by. In all banquets and feasts they are shown the greatest honour: they are placed at the upper end of the table, where they are the first served: at the lower end, they help the men. All the rest of their time they employ in walking or riding, in playing at cards or otherwise, in visiting their friends and keeping company, conversing with their equals (whom they term, gossips) and their neighbours, and making merry with them at childbirths, christenings, churchings [church social events] and funerals; and all this with the permission and knowledge of their husbands, as such is the custom. Although the husbands often recommend to them the pains, industry and care of the German or Dutch women, who do what the men ought to do both in the house and the shop, for which services in England men are employed, nevertheless the women usually persist in retaining their customs. This is why England is called the paradise of married women.

Van Meteren, "The Paradise of Married Women," *Nederlandische Historie* (1575), in W.B. Rye, *England as Seen by Foreigners* (1865).

Marriage and Children

In the following excerpt, philosopher and writer Francis Bacon discusses the positive and negative aspects of marriage and child rearing during Elizabeth's time. He explains that getting married and having children provide numerous joys but that the job of child rearing is time-consuming. Therefore, he believes that some occupations should be left to those who are childless.

He that hath wife and children hath given hostages to fortune [limited his chances in life]; for they are impediments to great enterprises, either of virtue or mischief. Certainly, the best works, and of greatest merit for the public, have proceeded from unmarried or childless men, which both in affection and means have married and endowed the public. Yet it were great reason that those that have children should have greatest care of future times, unto which they know they must transmit their dearest pledges. . . . A single life doth well with churchmen, for charity will hardly water the ground where it must first fill a pool. . . . Certainly, wife and children are a kind of discipline of humanity; and single men, though they be many times more charitable, because their means are less exhaust[ed], yet, on the other side, they are more cruel and hard-hearted (good to make severe inquisitors), because their tenderness is not so often called upon. . . . Wives are young men's mistresses; companions for middle age; and old men's nurses. So as a man may have a quarrel to marry when he will. But yet he was reputed one of the wise men, that made answer to the question, when a man should marry: A young man not yet, an older man not at all.

The joys of parents are secret, and so are their griefs and fears: they cannot utter the one, nor they will not utter the other. Children sweeten labours, but they make misfortunes more bitter: they increase the cares of life, but they mitigate the remembrance of death.

Francis Bacon, *Essays* (1597).

A Country Wedding

In this excerpt, ballad writer and journalist Thomas Deloney describes a typical upper-class wedding; in this case, the bride is a young woman whose family lives on a large estate near a country village. Deloney describes the guests, the bride's attire, the wedding procession to the church, and the ten-day celebration that follows.

The family unit was a close-knit structure in the upper strata of Elizabethan society, as this portrait of a wealthy family suggests.

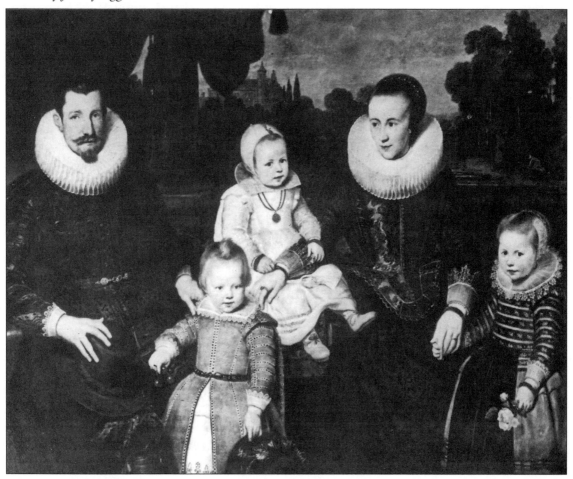

So the marriage day being appointed, all things . . . [ready] for the wedding, and royal cheer ordained, most of the lords, knights and gentlemen thereabout were invited thereunto; the bride being attired in a gown of sheep's russet and a kirtle [skirt] of fine worsted [fine wool], her head attired with a biliment [ornament] of gold, and her hair as yellow as gold hanging down behind her, which was curiously combed and plaited according to the manner of those days. She was led to church between two sweet boys, with bride-laces and rosemary tied about their silken sleeves: the one of them was son to Sir Thomas Parry, the other to Sir Francis Hungerford. Then was there a fair bride-cup of silver and gilt carried before her, hung about with silken ribbons of all colours; next was there a noise [group] of musicians, that played all the way before her; after her came all the chiefest maidens of the country, some bearing great bridecakes and some garlands of wheat finely gilded, and so she passed unto the church. . . .

The marriage being solemnised [vows spoken], home they came in order as before, and to dinner they went, where was no want of good cheer, no lack of melody: Rhenish [from the Rhine Valley] wine at this wedding was as plentiful as beer or ale, for the merchants had sent thither ten tuns [casks of wine] of the best in the Steelyard [storehouse in London].

This wedding endured ten days, to the great relief of the poor that dwelt all about; and in the end the bride's father and moth-

This seventeenth-century portrait of a young married couple depicts the bond shared by husband and wife.

er came to pay their daughter's portion [dowry], which when the bridegroom had received, he gave them great thanks . . .

Thomas Deloney, *Jacke of Newberie* (1597).

Men's and Women's Fashions

Fashion was important to upper-class Eliza-bethans. In this excerpt, historian William Harrison describes the types of clothing men and women like. He also complains that men's fashions have become much too expensive, while women's fashions are too immodest and revealing.

This contemporary painting portrays an array of upper-class fashions of Elizabethan England. The men and women of the age were very clothes conscious.

The fantastical folly [wild clothes] of our nation, even from the courtier to the carter, is such that no form of apparel liketh [pleases] us longer than the first garment is in the wearing, if it continue so long and be not laid aside, to receive some other trinket newly devised by the fickle-headed tailors, who covet to have several tricks in cutting, thereby to draw fond customers to more expense of money. For my part, I can tell better how to inveigh against this enormity than describe any certainty of our attire; since such is our muta-

bility that today there is none to [nothing comparable to] the Spanish guise, tomorrow the French toys [trinkets] are most fine and delectable, ere long no such apparel as [except] that which is after the high Alman [German] fashion, by and by the Turkish manner is generally best liked of, otherwise the Morisco [Moorish] gowns, the Barbarian sleeves, the mandilion [a cape with sleeves] worn to Colley-Weston-ward, and the short French breeches make such a comely vesture that, except it were a dog in a doublet, you shall not see any so disguised as are my countrymen of England. And as these fashions are diverse, so likewise it is a world to see the costliness and the curiosity, the excess and the vanity, the pomp and the bravery [splendor], the change and the variety, and finally the fickleness and the folly, that is in all degrees, insomuch that nothing is more constant in England than inconstancy of attire. Oh, how much cost is bestowed nowadays upon our bodies, and how little upon our souls! How many suits of apparel hath the one, and how little furniture hath the other! How long time is asked in decking up of the first, and how little space left wherein to feed the latter! How curious [hard to satisfy], how nice [fastidious] also, are a number of men and women, and how hardly can the tailor please them in making it fit for their bodies! How many times must it be sent back again to him that made it! What chafing, what fretting, what reproachful language doth the poor workman bear away! And many times when he doth nothing to it at all, yet when it is brought home again, it is very fit and handsome; then must we put it on, then must the long seams of our hose be set by a plumb-line, then we puff, then we blow, and finally, sweat till we drop, that our clothes may stand well upon us. . . .

In women also it is most to be lamented that they do now far exceed the lightness [lasciviousness] of our men (who nevertheless are transformed from the cap even to the very shoe), and such staring attire as in time past was supposed meet for none but light hussies only, is now become an habit for chaste and sober matrons.

What should I say of their doublets with pendant codpieces on the breast, full of jags and cuts, and sleeves of sundry colors? their galligaskins [loose breeches] to bear out their bums and make their attire to fit plum round (as they term it) about them? their farthingales [hoop skirts] and diversely colored nether stocks of silk, jersey, and such like, whereby their bodies are rather deformed than commended? I have met with some of these trulls [loose women] in London so disguised, that it hath passed my skill to discern whether they were men or women.

William Harrison, *The Description of England* (1587).

The Work of a Farmer's Wife

In the following excerpt, Justice Anthony Fitzherbert catalogs the duties of a farmer's wife during Elizabethan times.

And when thou [the farmer's wife] art up and ready, then first sweep thy house, dress up thy dishboard, and set all things in good order within thy house. Milk thy kie [cows], suckle thy calves, sile up [strain] thy milk, take up thy children and array them, and provide for thy husband's breakfast, dinner, supper, and for thy children and servants; and take thy part with them. And . . . ordain [set aside a portion of] corn [grain] and malt to the mill to bake and brew withal when need is. And mete [measure] it to the mill and from the mill, and see that thou have thy measure again besides the toll [charges] or else the miller dealeth not truly with thee, or else thy corn is not dry as it should be. Thou must make butter and cheese when thou may. Serve thy swine both morning and evening, and give thy pullen [poultry] meat [food] in the morning. And when time of year cometh, thou must take heed how thy hens, ducks, and geese do lay, and to gather up their eggs. . . .

And in the beginning of March, or a little before, is time for a wife to make her garden and to get as many good seeds and herbs as she can, and specially such as be good for the pot and for to eat. And as oft as need shall require, it must be weeded, for else the weed will overgrow the herbs. And also in March is time to sow flax [a plant used to make linen] and hemp [a plant used to make rope]. . . . But how it should be sown, weeded, pulled, rippled [combed], watered, washed, dried, beaten, braked [crushed], tawed [softened], hackled [hacked], spun, wound, wrapped, and woven, it needed not for me to show, for they [wives] be wise enough. And thereof may they make sheets, boardcloths [tablecloths], towels, shirts, smocks, and such other necessaries. And therefore let thy distaff [a staff used in spinning] be always ready for a pastime that thou be not idle. . . .

It is a wife's occupation to winnow [to separate chaff from grain] all manner of corns, to make malt [for brewing beer], wash and wring, to make hay, to shear corn, and in time of need to help her husband to fill the muck wain [farm wagon] or dung cart, drive the plow, to load hay, corn, and such other. Also to go or ride to the market to sell butter, cheese, milk, eggs, chickens, capons [male chickens], hens, pigs, geese, and all manner of corn. And also to buy all manner of necessary things belonging to a household, and to make a true reckoning and account to her husband what she hath received and what she hath paid. And if the husband go to the market to buy or sell (as they oft do), he then to show his wife in like manner. For if one of them should use [practice] to deceive the other, he deceiveth himself, and he is not like to thrive, and therefore they must be true either to other.

Anthony Fitzherbert, *The Book of Husbandry* (1523).

A Dictionary of Rogues

In 1561 historian John Awdeley compiled a list of rogues, or dishonorable people, who wandered the countryside and villages looking for ways to steal money from the weak and innocent. In the following excerpt, Awdeley identifies several categories of rogues and describes their appearance and practices.

An Abram-man.

An abram-man is he that walketh bare-armed, and bare-legged, and feigneth himself mad [pretends to be crazy], and carryeth a pack of wool, or a stick with bacon on it, or suchlike toy, and nameth himself Poor Tom.

A highwayman robs a nobleman's carriage. The Elizabethan countryside was not a safe place to travel.

A Ruffler.

A ruffler goeth with a weapon to seek service, saying he hath been a servitor in the wars, and beggeth for his relief. But his chiefest trade is to rob poor wayfaring men and market women.

A Prigman.

A prigman goeth with a stick in his hand like an idle person. His property is to steal clothes of the hedge, which they call storing of the rogueman; or else filch poultry, carrying them to the ale-house, which they call the bousing inn, and there sit playing at cards and dice, till that is spent which they have so filched.

A Whip-jack.

A whip-jack is one, that by colour of a counterfeit licence (which they call a gybe, and the seals they call jarks) doth use to beg like a mariner; but his chiefest trade is to rob booths in a fair, or to pilfer ware from stalls, which they call heaving of the booth.

A Frater.

A frater goeth with a like licence to beg for some spital-house [a hospital for patients with contagious diseases] or hospital. Their prey is commonly upon poor women as they go and come to the markets.

A Queer-bird.

A queer-bird is one that came lately out of prison and goeth to seek service. He is commonly a stealer of horses, which they [common people] term a prigger of palfreys. . . .

A Palliard.

A palliard is he that goeth in a patched cloak; and his doxy [a prostitute] goeth in like apparel.

An Irish Toyle.

An Irish toyle is he that carrieth his ware in his wallet, as laces, pins, points and suchlike. He useth to show no wares until he have his alms [money]; and if the goodman and wife be not in the way, he procureth of the children or servants a fleece of wool, or the worth of twelve pence of some other thing, for a penny-worth of his wares.

A Jarkman.

A jarkman is he that can write and read, and sometime speak Latin. He useth to make counterfeit licences which they call gybes, and sets to seals, in their language called jarks.

A Swigman.

A swigman goeth with a pedlar's pack.

A Washman.

A washman is called a palliard, but not of the right making. He useth to lie in the highway with lame or sore legs or arms to beg. These men the right pal-liards will oftentimes spoil, but they dare not complain. They be bitten with spick-worts and sometime with ratsbane [rat poison]. . . .

A Kitchin Morts.

A kitchin morts is a girl; she is brought at her full age to the uprightman to be bro-ken, and so she is called a doxy until she come to the honour of an altham [wife].

Doxies.

Note especially all which go abroad work-ing laces and shirt-strings. They name them doxies.

John Awdeley, *The Fraternity of Vagabonds both ruffling and beggarly, Men and Women, Boys and Girls, with their proper names and qualities* (1561).

The Condition of English Inns

In the following excerpt, writer William Harrison explains that Elizabethan travel-ers were at great risk of being robbed. Often the thieves included employees at the inn— among them, the inn's horseman, tapster (bartender), and chamberlain (housekeep-er)—who slyly assessed the traveler's belong-ings, compared notes, and made plans to steal. Travelers had a hard time escaping these practices.

Many an honest man is spoiled [robbed] of his goods as he traveleth to and fro, in which feat also the counsel of the tapsters or draw-ers of drink and chamberlains is not seldom behind or wanting. Certes [certainly] I believe not that chapman [merchant] or traveler in England is robbed by the way without the knowledge of some of them [inn employees]; for when he cometh into the inn, and alighteth from his horse, the hostler forthwith is very busy to take down his budget [leather pouch] or capcase [small traveling bag] in the yard from his saddle-bow, which he peiseth [weighs] slyly in his hand to feel the weight thereof: or if he miss of this pitch [trick], when the guest hath taken up his chamber, the chamberlain [maid] that looketh to the making of the beds will be sure to remove it from the place where the owner hath set it, as if it were to set it more conveniently somewhere else, whereby he getteth an inkling whether it be money or other short wares [less valuable things], and thereof giveth warning to such odd guests as haunt the house and are of his confederacy [conspiracy], to the utter undoing of many an honest yeoman as he journeyeth by the way. The tapster in like sort for his part doth mark his behavior and what plenty of money he draweth when he payeth the shot [bill] to the like end, so that it shall be a hard matter to escape all their subtle practices.

William Harrison, *The Description of England* (1587).

The Horse Stealer from Cornwall

In the following passage, Robert Greene, a playwright and journalist, tells the story of a horse thief in Cornwall, in western England, who stole a black horse from a gentleman, resold the horse to the same man, and wrote a letter telling the gentleman he had been fooled. Angry that the thief had fooled him, the gentleman saved the letter and later used it to convict the thief of horse stealing; ultimately, the thief was sentenced to death.

Not far from T[ru]ro in Cornwall, a certain prigger, a horse-stealer, being a lance-man [armed thief], surveying the pastures thereabouts, spied a fair black horse without any white spot at all about him. The horse was fair and lusty [energetic], well proportioned, of a high crest [neck], of a lusty countenance [appearance], well buttocked, and strongly trussed [built], which set the prigger's teeth a water [the prigger wanted] to have him. Well, he knew the hardest hap was but a halter [best chance to take the horse by the halter], and therefore he ventured fair, and stole away the prancer; and, seeing his stomach was so good as his limbs, he kept him well, and by his policy seared him [burned a spot] in the forehead, and made him spotted in the back, as if he had been saddle-bitten [sores from a rubbing saddle], and gave him a mark in both ears, whereas he had but a mark in one.

Dealing thus with his horse, after a quarter of a year, that all hurly-burly [confusion] was past for the horse, he came riding to T[ru]ro to the market, and there offered him to be sold. The gentleman that lost the horse was there present, and looking on him with other gentlemen, liked him passing well, and commended him, insomuch that he bet the price of him, bargained, and bought him. And so when he was tolled [charged], and the horse-stealer clapped him good luck: "Well, my friend," quoth the gentleman, "I like the horse the better, in that once I lost one, as like him as might be, but mine wanted [did not have] these saddle spots and this star in the forehead."—"It may be so, sir," said the prigger. And so the gentleman and he parted. The next day after, he [the thief] caused a letter to be made, and sent the gentleman word that he had his horse again that he lost, only he had given him a mark or two, and for that he was well rewarded, having twenty mark for his labour. The gentleman, hearing how he was cozened [tricked] by a horse-stealer, and not only robbed, but mocked, let it pass till he might conveniently meet with him to revenge it.

It fortuned, not long after, that this lance-man prigger was brought to T[ru]ro jail for some such matter, and indeed it was about a mare that he had stolen. But as knaves have friends, especially when they are well moneyed, he found divers [several] that spake for him, and who said it was the first fault, and the party plaintiff gave but slender evidence against him, so that the judge spake favourably in his behalf. The gentleman as then sat on the bench, and, calling to mind the prigger's countenance, how he had stolen his horse and mocked him, remembered he had the letter in his pocket that he sent him, and therefore, rising up, spake in his behalf, and highly commended the man, and desired the judges for one fault he might not be cast away.

"And, besides, may it please you," quoth he, "I had this morning a certificate of his honesty and good behaviour sent me"; and with that he delivered them the letter, and the Judge, with the rest of the bench, smiled at this conceit [image], and asked the fellow if he never stole horse from that gentleman.

"No," quoth the prigger, "I know him not. Your honours mistakes me."

Said the gentleman, "He did borrow [steal] a black horse of me, and marked him with a star in the forehead, and asked twenty mark of me for his labour"; and so discoursed [explained] the whole matter. Whereupon the quest went upon him, and condemned him, and so the prigger went to Heaven in a string [right away], as many of his faculty had done before.

Robert Greene, *The Second Part of Cony-Catching* (1591).

The Black Art of Lock Picking

In the following excerpt, playwright and journalist Robert Greene describes the skill of lock pickers. Lock pickers were skilled thieves who worked very quickly. For this reason, Greene imagines that they must be working with a satanic power.

The black art is picking of locks; and to this busy trade two persons are required, the charm and the stand. The charm is he that doth the feat, and the stand is he that watcheth. There be more that do belong to the burglary for conveying away the goods, but only two are employed about the lock. The charm hath many keys and wrests [small tools], which they call picklocks, and for every sundry fashion they have a sundry term; but I am ignorant of their words of art, and therefore I omit them: only this, they have such cunning in opening a lock, that they will undo the hardest lock though never so well warded [guarded], even while a man may turn his back. Some have their instruments from Italy, made of steel; some are made here by smiths, that are partakers in their villainous occupations. But, howsoever, well may it be called the black art, for the Devil cannot do better than they in their faculty. . . .

I once saw the experience of it myself, for, being in the Counter upon commandment, there came in a famous fellow in the black art, as strong in that quality as Samson. The party now is dead, and by fortune died in his bed. I, hearing that he was a charm, began to enter familiarity with him, and to have an insight into his art. After some acquaintance he told me much, and one day, being in my chamber, I showed him my desk, and asked him if he could pick that little lock that was so well warded, and too little, as I thought, for any of his gins [tools].

"Why, sir," says he, "I am so experienced in the black art, that if I do but blow upon the lock, it shall fly open; and therefore let me come to your desk, and do but turn five times about, and you shall see my cunning." With that I did as he bade me, and ere I had turned five times, his hand was rifling in my desk very orderly. I wondered at it, and thought verily that the Devil and his dam was in his fingers. Much discommodity [household articles] grows by this black art in shops and noblemen's houses for their plate. Therefore are they [lock pickers] most severely to be looked into by the honourable and worshipful of England.

Robert Greene, *The Second and last part of Conny-catching.* London: William Wright, 1597.

Hanging was a common form of punishment in the Elizabethan age. Here, three women are hanged on suspicion of witchcraft.

Crimes and Punishments

Punishments for crimes in Elizabethan England were usually swift and severe. In the following excerpt, historian William Harrison describes some of the punishments criminals might face, including branding, hanging, or being drawn and quartered.

The greatest and most grievous punishment used in England, for such as offend against the state, is drawing from the prison to the place of execution upon an hurdle or sled, where they [the criminals] are hanged till they be half dead, and then taken down and quartered; after that, their members and bowels are cut from their bodies, and thrown into a fire provided near hand and within their own sight, even for the same purpose. Sometimes, if the trespass be not the more heinous, they are suffered to hang till they be quite dead. And whensoever any of the nobility are convicted of high treason, this manner of their death is converted into the loss of their heads only, notwithstanding that the sentence do run after the former order. . . .

Under the word felony are many grievous crimes contained, as: breach of prison [escape], disfigurers of the prince's liege people; hunting by night with painted faces and visors [masks]; rape, or stealing of women and maidens; conspiracy against the person of the prince; embezzling of goods committed by the master to the servant, above the value of forty shillings; carrying of horses or mares into Scotland; sodomy and buggery [illegal sex]; stealing of hawks' eggs; conjuring, sorcery, witchcraft and digging up of crosses; prophesying upon arms, cognisances [crests], names and badges [emblems]; casting of slanderous bills; wilful killing of a soldier from the field; departure of a soldier from the field; diminution of coin, all offences within case of *praemunire* [appealing to or obeying a foreign court or authority], embezzling of records, goods taken from dead men by their servants, stealing of whatsoever cattle, robbing by the highway, upon the sea, or of dwelling houses, letting out of ponds, cutting of purses, stealing of deer by night, counterfeiters of coin. . . . Perjury is punished by the pillory, burning in the forehead with the letter P, and loss of all his moveables [limbs].

Many trespasses also are punished by the cutting of one or both ears from the head of the offender, as the utterance of seditious words against the magistrates, fray-makers [those starting brawls], petty robbers, etc. Rogues are burned through the ears; carriers of sheep out of the land, by the loss of their hands; such as kill by poison are either scalded to death in lead or seething water.

Heretics are burned quick; harlots and their mates, by carting, ducking and doing of open penance in sheets [draped costume], in churches and market steads, are often put to rebuke. . . . The dragging of some of them over the Thames between Lambeth and Westminster at the tail of a boat, is a punishment that most terrifieth them which are condemned thereto. . . .

Rogues and vagabonds are often stocked [put in stocks] and whipped; scolds are ducked upon cucking-stools [a chair to which an offender is tied] in the water. Such felons as stand mute, and speak not at their arraignment, are pressed to death by huge weights laid upon a board that lieth over their breast, and a sharp stone under their backs, and these commonly hold their peace thereby to save their goods unto their wives and children, which, if they were condemned, should be confiscated to the prince. Thieves that are saved by their books and clergy [proving themselves literate] are burned in the left hand, upon the brawn [fleshy part] of the thumb, with an hot iron, so that if they be apprehended again that mark bewrayeth them to have been arraigned of felony before, whereby they are sure at that time to have no mercy. . . .

William Harrison, *Description of England* (1587).

Witches and Their Craft

Writer and member of Parliament Reginald Scot wrote The Discovery of Witchcraft *to prevent the persecution of poor and old people believed to be witches. Witchcraft was a capi-*

tal offense in England from 1542 to 1547 and from 1563 to 1736. During these periods about a thousand witches were executed. In this excerpt from Scot's book, the author describes what witches look like and what they do.

One sort of such as are said to be witches are women which be commonly old, lame, blear-eyed, pale, foul, and full of wrinkles; poor, sullen, superstitious, and papists [Catholics], or such as know no religion, in whose drowsy minds the devil hath got a fine seat, so as what mischief, mischance, calamity or slaughter is brought to pass, they are easily persuaded the same is done by themselves, imprinting in their minds an earnest and constant imagination hereof. They are lean and deformed, showing melancholy in their faces, to the horror of all that see them. They are doting scolds, mad, devilish, and not much differing from them that are thought to be possessed with spirits. So firm and steadfast in their opinions as whosoever shall only have respect to the constancy of their words uttered would easily believe they were true indeed.

These miserable wretches are so odious unto all their neighbors and so feared as few dare offend them or deny them anything they ask, whereby they take upon them, yea and sometimes think, that they can do such things such as are beyond the ability of human nature. These go from house to house and from door to door for a pot full of milk, yeast, drink, pottage [stew] or some such relief, without the which they could hardly live. . . .

And further, in tract of time the witch waxeth [becomes more] odious and tedious to her neighbors, and they again are despised and despited of her, so as sometimes she curseth one and sometimes another, and that from the master of the house, his wife, children, cattle, &c., to the little pig that lieth in the sty. Thus in process of time they have all displeased her, and she hath wished evil luck unto them all, perhaps with curses and imprecations made in form. Doubtless (at length) some of her neighbors die, or fall sick, or some of their children are visited with diseases that vex them strangely, as apoplexies, epilepsies, convulsions, hot fevers, worms, &c., which by ignorant parents are supposed to be the vengeance of witches. . . .

The witch, on the other side, expecting her neighbor's mischances and seeing things come to pass according to her wishes, curses, and incantations (for [French philosopher Jean] Bodin himself confesseth that not above two in a hundred of their witchings or wishings take effect) being called before a justice, by due examination of the circumstances is driven to see her imprecations and desires and her neighbor's harms and losses to concur and as it were to take effect and so confesseth that she (as a goddess) hath brought such things to pass. . . .

Reginald Scot, *The Discovery of Witchcraft* (1584).

Creatures of Folklore

Belief that fairies, spirits, and other magical creatures could surprise, frighten, or harm people was widespread in Elizabethan

England. Here, writer and member of Parliament Reginald Scot catalogs the names of these fearful spirits and explains that cowardly people and those terrified by scary stories in their childhood are most likely to be frightened by these creatures.

But certainly, some one knave [crafty person] in a white sheet hath cozened [tricked] and abused many thousands that way, specially when Robin Goodfellow [a fairy] kept such a coil [fuss] in the country. But you shall understand that these bugs [any folklore creature to be feared] specially are spied and feared of sick folk, children, women, and cowards which through weakness of mind and body are shaken with vain dreams and continual fear. The Scythians [East Europeans], being a stout and warlike nation (as divers [various] writers report), never see any vain sights or spirits. It is a common saying, a lion feareth no bugs. But in our childhood our mother's maids have so terrified us with an ugly devil having horns on his head, fire in his mouth, and a tail in his breech [buttocks], eyes like a basin, fangs like a dog, claws like a bear, a skin like a Niger [from West Africa], and a voice roaring like a lion, whereby we start and are afraid when we hear one cry, "Boo"; and they have so affrayed [frightened] us with bull beggars, spirits, witches, urchins, elves, hags, fairies, satyrs, pans, fauns, silens, kit-with-a-canstick [jack-o'-lanterns], tritons, centaurs, dwarfs, giants, imps, calcars, conjurers, nymphs, changelings, incubus, Robin Goodfellow, the spoorne, the mare, the man in the oak, the hell wain [wagon], the firedrake [dragon],

the puckle, Tom Thumb [tiny person of folklore], hobgoblin, Tom Tumbler, boneless, and such other bugs, that we are afraid of our own shadows. In so much as some never fear the devil but in a dark night, and then a polled sheep is a perilous beast and many times is taken for our father's soul, specially in a churchyard, where a right hardy man heretofore scant durst [hardly dares] pass by night but his hair would stand upright. . . .

Reginald Scot, *The Discovery of Witchcraft* (1584).

Magical Home Remedies

Historian Thomas Hill collected folklore tales explaining how people could practice magic at home, either for entertainment or as solutions to mysterious problems. In the following examples from his collection, Hill recommends methods to conjure both nightmares and pleasant dreams and suggests several ways to rid one's bedroom of fleas.

To Make One See Fearful Sights in His Sleep:

And to do this, take the blood of a lapwing and therewith anoint the pulses of thy forehead before thy going to rest, and then after in thy sleep thou shalt see both marvellous and fearful sights, as Vitalis Medicus [poet of life] writeth. Also he writeth, that if a man eateth in the evening before his going to bed of the herb named nightshade, or mandrake, or henbane, shall after see in his sleep pleasant sights.

How to Kill Fleas Divers [Several] Ways:

And first to gather all the fleas of thy chamber into one place, anoint a staff with the grease of a fox or hedgehog, and lay the staff again where you list [choose] in your chamber, and it shall so gather all the fleas by it. Also fill a dish with goat's blood, and set the same by the bed, and all the fleas will come to it round about. And the like will they do by the blood of the hedgehog.

Thomas Hill, *Naturall and Artificiall Conclusions* (1567).

The Buzzing London Streets

In Elizabeth's day, London streets were busy, crowded, and noisy. Here, playwright and journalist Thomas Dekker describes a street scene.

In every street, carts and coaches make such a thundering as if the world ran upon wheels; at every corner, men, women and children meet in such shoals [crowds], that posts are set up of purpose to strengthen the houses, lest with jostling one another they should shoulder them down. Besides, hammers are beating in one place, tubs hooping [putting hoops on barrels] in another, pots clinking in a third, water-tankards [water-carts] running at tilt in a fourth. Here are porters sweating under burdens, there merchants' men bearing bags of money. Chapmen (as if they were at leap-frog) skip out of one shop into

Thomas Dekker (pictured) was a renowned Elizabethan playwright and journalist.

another. Tradesmen (as if they were dancing galliards) are lusty at legs and never stand still. All are as busy as country attorneys at assizes [court sessions].

Thomas Dekker, *The Seven Deadly Sinnes of London* (1606).

A Survey of London Shopkeepers

In 1598 historian John Stow compiled the Survey of London, *an account of the way the city looked. In the following excerpt from the* Survey, *Stow lists the many different types of shops and shopkeepers in London and in what areas of the city they can be found.*

Stow's Survey *shows that, despite the often chaotic appearance of Elizabethan London, there were some orderly arrangements; for example, shops selling similar wares were often located together on the same street.*

Men of trades and sellers of wares in this city [London] have often times since changed their places, as they have found their best advantage. For whereas mercers [dealers in expensive cloth] and haberdashers used to keep their shops in West Cheap, of later time they held them on London Bridge, where partly they yet remain. The goldsmiths of Guthertons [Gutter] Lane and Old Exchange are now for the most part removed into the south side of West Cheap, the pepperers and grocers of Sopers Lane are now in Bucklesbury, and other places. The drapers [dealers in cloth] of Lombard Street and of Cornhill are seated in Candlewick Street and Watheling Street; the skinners [one who sells animal skins] from St. Mary Pellipers, or at the Axe, into Budge Row and Walbrooke; the stockfishmongers [sellers of dried fish] in Thames Street; wet fishmongers in Knightriders Street and Bridge Street; the ironmongers, of Ironmongers Lane and Old Jewry, into Thames Street; the vintners from the Vinetree [Vintry] into divers [various] places. But the brewers for the more part remain near to the friendly water of Thames; the butchers in Eastcheap and St. Nicholas Shambles; the hosiers [makers or sellers of stockings] of old time in Hosier Lane, near unto Smithfield, are since removed into Cordwainer Street, the upper part thereof by Bow Church, and last of all into Birchoveris [Birchin] Lane by Cornhill; the shoemakers and curriers of Cordwainer Street removed, the one to St. Martins le Grand, the other to London Wall near unto Moorgate; the founders [casters of metal] remain by themselves in Lothbury; cooks or pastlers [bakers] for the more part in Thames Street, the other dispersed into divers parts; poulterers of late removed out of the Poultry betwixt the stocks and great conduit in Cheap, into Grass Street and St. Nicholas Shambles; bowyers [bow makers], from Bowyers Row by Ludgate into divers places, and almost worn out with the fletchers [arrow makers]; Pater Noster bead-makers and text-writers are gone out of Pater Noster Row into Stationers [booksellers' area] of Pauls Churchyard; patten makers [makers of clogs or overshoes] of St. Margaret, Pattens Lane, clean worn out; laborers every workday are to be found in Cheap, about Sopers Lane end; horse coursers [dealers or brokers] and sellers of oxen, sheep, swine, and such like, remain in their old market of Smithfield, etc.

John Stow, *Survey of London* (1598).

London Bridge

In the sixteenth century, London Bridge was the only bridge crossing the Thames River. It connected the capital city to the countryside beyond. The bridge was also a neighborhood; many shops and houses were built on it. The following excerpt from a book entitled An Itinerary *by a little-known writer named Fynes Moryson describes the bridge and the houses built upon it.*

The bridge at London is worthily to be numbered among the miracles of the world, if men respect the building and foundation laid artificially and stately over an ebbing and flowing water upon 21 piles of stone, with 20 arches, under which barks [ships] may pass, the lowest foundation being (as they say) packs of wool, most durable against the force of water, and not to be repaired but upon great fall of the waters and by artificial turning or stopping the course of them; or if men respect the houses built upon the bridge, as great and high as those of the firm land, so as a man cannot know that he passeth a bridge, but would judge himself to be in the street, save that the houses on both sides are combined in the top, making the passage somewhat dark, and that in some few open places the river of Thames may be seen on both sides.

Fynes Moryson, *An Itinerary* (1617).

A drawing captures London Bridge as it appeared during the reign of Queen Elizabeth. More than a bridge spanning the Thames River, London Bridge was a neighborhood with a number of shops and houses.

Brothels in London's Suburbs

Houses of prostitution, called brothels, were common in Elizabethan London. In the following excerpt, writer Thomas Nashe attacks the brothel owners and the prostitutes who work in them. He accuses government officials of taking bribes to allow brothels to operate and prostitutes of picking the pockets of their clients. He also calls on government officials to stop the trade.

London, what are thy suburbs but licensed stews [brothels]? Can it be so many brothel-houses of salary sensuality and sixpenny whoredom (the next door to the magistrate's) should be set up and maintained, if bribes did not bestir them? I accuse none, but certainly justice somewhere is corrupted. Whole hospitals of ten-times-a-day dishonested strumpets have we cloistered together. Night and day the entrance unto them is as free as to a tavern. Not one of them but hath a hundred retainers [gathered clients]. Prentices and poor servants they [prostitutes] encourage to rob their masters. Gentlemen's purses and pockets they will dive into and pick, even whiles they are dallying with them.

No Smithfield ruffianly swashbuckler will come off with such harsh hell-raking oaths as they [the prostitutes]. Every one of them is a gentlewoman, and either the wife of two husbands or a bed-wedded bride before she was ten years old. The speech-shunning sores and sight-irking botches [ruin] of their unsatiate intemperance [limitless excesses] they will unblushingly lay forth and jestingly brag of whatever they haunt. To church they never repair. Not in all their whole life would they hear of GOD, if it were not for their huge swearing and forswearing by Him.

Great cunning do they ascribe to their art, as, the discerning by the very countenance [appearance] a man that hath crowns in his purse; the fine closing in with the next Justice, or Alderman's deputy of the ward;

A portrait of Mary Frith in male attire. Frith was one of the most notorious prostitutes of the Elizabethan age.

the winning love of neighbours round about to repel violence if haply their houses should be environed [beset], or any in them prove unruly. . . .

Awake your wits, grave authorised law-distributors, and show yourselves as insinuative-subtle in smoking this city-sodoming [illegal sex] trade out of his starting-hole as the professors of it are in underpropping it.

Thomas Nashe, *Christ's Tears over Jerusalem* (1593).

Laws Governing Brothels

In his Survey of London, *historian John Stow compiles a list of ordinances governing brothels. The laws, among other things, discourage the solicitation of women, protect religious days from the brothel's business, and require searches of brothels by law officials.*

In a Parliament holden at Westminster [Parliament buildings], the 8th of Henry the Second [in 1162], it was ordained by the commons, and confirmed by the king and lords, that divers [various] constitutions forever should be kept within that lordship or franchise, according to the old customs that had been there used time out of mind. Amongst the which these following were some, viz [for example]:

That no stewholder [brothel owner] or his wife should let [prevent] or stay any single woman to go and come freely at all times when they listed.

No stewholder to keep any woman to board, but she to board abroad at her pleasure.

To take no more for the woman's chamber in the week than fourteen pence [about $2.25].

Not to keep open his doors upon the holy days.

Not to keep any single woman in his house on the holy days. . . .

No single woman to be kept against her will that would leave her sin.

No stewholder to receive any woman of religion, or any man's wife.

No single woman to take money to lie with any man, but she lie with him all night till the morrow.

No man to be drawn or enticed into any stewhouse.

The constables, bailiff, and others, every week to search every stewhouse.

No stewholder to keep any woman that hath the perilous infirmity of burning [disease], nor to sell bread, ale, flesh, fish, wood, coal, or any victuals, etc.

These and many more orders were to be observed upon great pain and punishment.

John Stow, *Survey of London* (1598).

Index

Picture Credits

About the Editor

Clarice Swisher is a freelance writer and editor and a former English teacher. She taught English in Minnesota for several years before devoting full time to writing. She is the author or editor of more than twenty books, including *The Importance of Pablo Picasso, The Glorious Revolution,* and *Genetic Engineering,* published by Lucent Books, and *The Spread of Islam, William Faulkner,* and *John F. Kennedy,* published by Greenhaven Press. She lives in Saint Paul, Minnesota.